Two Righteous Men

Two Wicked Cities

Bible History that Echoes
with Truth for Today

SAM MASON

InspiringVoices®

Inspiring Voices books may be ordered through booksellers or by contacting:

Inspiring Voices
1663 Liberty Drive
Bloomington, IN 47403
www.inspiringvoices.com
844-686-9605

Scripture quotations taken from The Holy Bible, New International Version® NIV® Copyright © 1973 1978 1984 2011 by Biblica, Inc. TM. Used by permission. All rights reserved worldwide.

ISBN: 978-1-4624-1310-2 (sc)
ISBN: 978-1-4624-1311-9 (e)

Library of Congress Control Number: 2020916986

Print information available on the last page.

Inspiring Voices rev. date: 09/28/2023

Contents

Acknowledgments

God has called me to ministries of communication. In my lifetime I've served as a preacher, teacher, counselor, singer, songwriter, broadcaster, and in more recent years, an author. As to the latter calling, I must confess that I'm not one of those gifted writers for whom words flow quickly and easily.

My book writing projects start with inspiration from the Lord, then involve much prayer and extensive research. Putting the words on paper is usually slow and tedious. I write and rewrite over, and over, and over again. Accuracy and clarity are my primary goals, accompanied by the hope that my style might even be engaging. The process is meant to present the truths of God's Word in a way that will enlighten and motivate.

Even after untold hours of personal effort though, I still need the help of proof-readers. They not only uncover typos, spelling and grammatical errors I might have missed, they point out anything which they feel may be worded awkwardly or unclearly. They suggest information that perhaps should be added, subtracted, or changed. On top of all this, they often simply encourage me in my efforts.

For the last few books, my proof-readers have

consisted of the same faithful duo. Once more I'm filled with deep appreciation for their work. Many thanks to the love of my life, Carol Mason, and my dear friend and pastor, Dr. Darrel Waller. I trust that your labors in this area will not have been in vain. Your input has improved this book. Together we hope that *Two Righteous Men, Two Wicked Cities*, will make a positive difference in the lives of its readers, and those affected by their influence as well.

Introduction

I was immensely blessed to have grown up in a loving Christian home. Godly values were instilled and fond memories created during those formative years. Such benefits both enriched my early days, and laid the foundation for the rest of my life. I'm grateful to my father, mother, and paternal grandmother, whose common faith was passed on to me in that simple but special house along Bull Creek Road in the little community of Fawn Township, Pennsylvania. Even more so, I thank *the Lord Himself* for the powerful influence of that healthy spiritual environment. The blessings He bestowed upon me there were of such worth that they're far beyond any possible monetary or material value to which I might try to equate them.

I was only 5 years old, when my dad lost his job as yard foreman and weighmaster following the shutdown of the coal mine where he'd worked his entire career to that point. I didn't grasp it at the time, but I later came to realize what a difficult financial blow it had been for the family. It was their trust in God which ultimately brought them through it.

A few years earlier mom and dad had become Christians, and in the aftermath of the loss of his employment, they decided they wanted to do something for the Lord. "Mason's Christian Bookstore" was soon born out of that desire. It opened in late 1954 in the business district of the nearby borough of Tarentum.

Unfortunately, they weren't able to make a long-term go of it financially. My father eventually found work at a hardware store there in town. The only sizable physical remnant of those few months of operating Mason's Christian Bookstore leaned against the side wall of our garage for many years to come. It was the original neon sign which had hung out front. Still, my parents' labor for the Kingdom of God in that place had left a beneficial effect upon a number of lives, including my own. Plus, they spent the remainder of their earthly sojourn serving the Lord and touching lives in numerous other ways.

6 and 1/2 decades later I can still envision the scene that appeared before me when I peered through the glass at the front of the bookstore for a few moments during that memorable mid-century Christmas season. Snow flakes sparkled under the old-fashioned street and holiday lights as I viewed Sixth Avenue and much of downtown Tarentum from where I sat on the front display ledge. Mom had allowed my older sister, Leslie, and me to pick out our own Christmas gifts from the shelves of that little newly established place of business. Leslie chose a colorful illustrated children's Old Testament. I didn't know much about the Bible at that age, but I determined that I didn't want an *old* one of anything. I chose the same book type, but the edition I picked was based upon the *New* Testament.

Ever since then I've continued reading and re-reading the same Bible stories illustrated in both those books. Of course, I don't read the childhood versions anymore, but the essence of the narratives is nevertheless the same. *Funny thing...* although I've gained much divine truth from both Old and New Testament tales of the Creator, the Savior, the saints, and others, ironically I've found myself more often drawn to the stories in the 39 books which make up the *Old* Testament. Those sacred historical accounts have taught me much, and have frequently been the source of sermons and teachings I've shared with others.

Such is the case once more. This book you're about to read is a careful examination of the story of a pair of Old Testament saints, and a pair of Old Testament urban centers. They may be ancient entities, but their experiences provide a critical message for contemporary Christianity and modern America.

Like I once did as a 5-year old, many today are inclined to largely dismiss the Old Testament. It's books, though divinely inspired, were penned mostly under the Old Covenant. As Christians we live under the New Covenant, and therefore those 39 books at the front of our Bible are often considered by some to be basically irrelevant. The laws, commandments, principles, statements, and accounts recorded there are deemed to be somewhat, or even totally, inapplicable in our time.

Of course as Hebrews 7:22 tells us, the New Covenant is a "better" one than the Old Covenant. But that doesn't mean that the Old Covenant is worthless and useless. The goal of both is to reconcile human beings to God. The Old Covenant fell short because *we* fall short (see Romans 3:23). The Old Covenant was *not bad* simply because in our old fallen nature we *are bad*. Indeed, Romans 7:12

declares: "So then, the law is holy, and the commandment is holy, righteous, and good."

We're certainly grateful to be under the New Covenant through the blood of Christ the Spotless Lamb, yet there is still much we can and should learn from the Old Covenant and the Old Testament. The commands presented there, with some in the New Testament as well, are not provided for the purpose of condemning us. They're intended to give us a glimpse into the heart and nature of the Creator. They are a picture of what His character is like, and what He wants ours to be like as well. The natural man sees rules simply as unhappy restrictions. The spiritual man learns that they're necessary aids to understanding the Lord and experiencing the righteous and blessed life He intends for us to enjoy.

I remind you that the *Old* Testament volumes are the ones referred to over and over again as "Scripture" by the Lord Jesus and His Apostles throughout the *New* Testament. They did not consider these books to be irrelevant! The divine covenant under which God's people now live may have changed, but God Himself has not. His nature remains the same through all generations. What the Old Testament tells us about the character of the Lord is still true today. In it God the Father declares that He is unchanging. Malachi 3:6: "I the LORD do not change." In the New Testament the same is said of His Son, our Savior. "Jesus Christ is the same yesterday and today and forever" (Hebrews 13:8).

My prayer concerning the exposition of the Genesis accounts in this work before you is two-fold. First, I've asked God to help me discover His precise perspective on the issues involved, and to communicate His Word to you with integrity and clarity. Secondly, I pray that your spirit will be open to receive these relevant truths, as you seek to honestly hear the heart of God on the matter. As these prayers are answered, I believe this book can go on to have a righteous impact on both the church and the nation I love so deeply. May it be, Lord! May it be!

Chapter 1

The Road Back Home

Over the years I've seen three particular words appearing on various kinds of signs hanging from the walls of houses. Those displays may have been wooden, plastic, metal or cloth; large or small; professionally produced or homemade; painted, printed, or stitched in needlepoint. Yet whatever form they may take, they all evoke a certain undeniable longing in most of us. "Home Sweet Home." Home may be the house where you grew up, or it could be a place where you lived later in life. Your concept of home might be native to one of the aforementioned kind of houses, or to a local community. Perhaps for you home has no geographical location at all. It could be identified with the companionship of a certain special person or persons. In any case, home always involves loving relationships.

If you've had the misfortune of never experiencing a habitat where you felt warmth and acceptance, then such longings may be somewhat foreign to you. Should that be the story of your life, then my wish for you is that you find a true home, most especially in the arms of God.

Home sweet home is a reality which all of us were meant to know experientially… a reality with origins in the heart of the Creator.

So what is home meant to be for humanity? You'll discover the answer in the opening chapters of the book of beginnings: Genesis. The initial terrestrial location of home is known as the Garden of Eden. We can't pinpoint it's exact historical location, but we do know that it was a place of unimaginable beauty and tranquility. Don't make the mistake, however, of thinking that it was predominately the elegance of that natural setting which made it home. No, the primary distinguishing feature of mankind's original home was *sweet fellowship*, first with the Lord, then with other creatures, particularly other people.

No matter how blissful, no other past or current home on this planet could compare in bounty to the love, joy, and peace that permeated Eden's outpost. Though the word is inadequate when applied to the Almighty, still, as we start to discuss divine fellowship, we must say that God is *social*. He created people in His image as *social* beings also. Life is only worth living because of loving relationships. All other earthly pleasures pale in comparison. In fact, I don't believe true pleasure exists on this planet outside of the context of affectionate relationships. In that regard, Adam and Eve experienced the epitome of a life of pleasure. Theirs was the rich life… the original righteous life.

We don't know how long they enjoyed that archetypal home sweet home, but sin and rebellion eventually forced them out. You likely know the account of how Satan came in the body of a serpent and enticed the first humans to accept his lies and defy the authority of the God who made them and had loving communion with them. The multi-faceted curse of Genesis 3:14-19 fell upon mankind and all creation as a result.

"So the LORD God said to the serpent, 'Because you have done this, cursed are you above all the livestock and all the wild animals! You will crawl on your belly and you will eat dust all the days of your life. And I will put enmity between you and the woman, and between your offspring and hers; he will crush your head, and you will strike his heel.' To the woman he said, 'I will greatly increase your pains in childbearing; with pain you will give birth to children. Your desire will be for your husband, and he will rule over you.' To Adam he said, 'Because you listened to your wife and ate from the tree about which I commanded you, You must not eat of it, cursed is the ground because of you; through painful toil you will eat of it all the days of your life. It will produce thorns and thistles for you, and you will eat the plants of the field. By the sweat of your brow you will eat your food until you return to the ground, since from it you were taken; for dust you are and to dust you will return.'"

As listed in the Scripture verses above, there were a number of negative effects of that curse. Yet the worst by far was the loss of the uninhibited intimacy with the Lord that was intended to be ours from the beginning. That loss of sweet divine fellowship mankind suffered as a consequence of the sin of Adam and Eve, was so extensive and enduring that it was not until generations later that men even began to gather in groups to call on the name of the Lord.

The curse commenced a cascade of burgeoning evil and consequential judgments which took their toll upon the earth and its inhabitants. The ensuing chapters of Genesis record two more major catastrophes upon humanity and the earth in the wake of the curse. The sins of unbelief and disobedience had resulted in the loss of divine fellowship, and the spread of wickedness. Soon they would bring planetary and social destruction upon nearly all.

Yet in the midst of what are otherwise predominately dark centuries of human history, the glowing testimonies of three righteous individuals of note engender hope for the future. Not coincidentally, this same trio leads the list of Faith's Hall of Fame heroes and heroines in Hebrews chapter 11. Their names? Abel, Enoch, and Noah.

The story of the first hero of the faith is unfortunately also the account of the world's first murder. Tragically, it involved one of the sons of Adam and Eve attacking and killing the other. Jealousy appeared to be the motive. Those first parents must have suffered incredible grief. They had experienced history's first human death, and as a result had suffered the loss of one of their own sons. In addition to *grief* over the untimely demise of one son and the murderous rage of another, *guilt* must have once again gripped their souls. After all, their original sin had opened the floodgate of evil that had allowed a wicked torrent to sweep away Cain and Abel. One was sentenced to be a restless wanderer after committing a treacherous homicide, the other suffered a premature and undeserved death.

Before his passing, however, Scripture reveals that "The LORD looked with favor on Abel and his offering..." (Genesis 4:4). On the other hand, it tells us "...but on Cain and his offering he did not look with favor. So Cain was very angry, and his face was downcast" (Genesis 4:5). We're not given the specifics of why Abel's sacrifice was pleasing to God and Cain's was not, but Hebrews 11:4 establishes the foundational difference between the brothers and their offerings. "By *faith* Abel offered God a better sacrifice than Cain did. By *faith* he was commended as a righteous man, when God spoke well of his offerings. And by *faith* he still speaks, even though he is dead." His enduring testimony proclaims God's love for Abel, and Abel's love for God.

Faith's Hall of Fame member number two teaches us that even in the darkest night of sin, individuals can return to a rich, rewarding fellowship with God. In the midst of a somewhat matter-of-fact genealogy, we encounter a very intriguing notation. Not much detail is given, but this single sentence stirs the heart, and once more provides another glimmer of hope for the future of mankind. "Enoch walked with God; then he was no more, because God took him away" (Genesis 5:24). As was the case with Abel, in Hebrews 11 we're informed that Enoch's *faith* was what made him pleasing to the Lord.

I once heard a preacher suggest that this early saint's departure from earth may have simply happened like this: "One day the Lord and Enoch traveled a little longer than usual on their daily stroll together, so God said to the man, 'Enoch, we're closer to my place than yours, why don't you just come home with Me?'" Yes, only one verse is all that Genesis devotes to his life of more than three and a half centuries, but that verse is an extremely short story with an extremely happy ending!

We initially learn of the final member of this opening trio of Faith's Hall of Famers in the closing verses of Genesis chapter 5. There we're offered a prophetic introduction to the righteous man who would become the hero of the first of the two "post-curse" population-wide calamities we mentioned earlier. There's a good chance you originally heard about Noah in a Sunday school class while you were a child. His is one of the Bible's most well-known stories.

Genesis 5:29 records that Noah's father, Lamech, gave him that name (meaning "rest") with an explanation which followed. "He will comfort us in the labor and painful toil of our hands caused by the ground the LORD has cursed." Noah would become the one righteous man who would prevent the extermination of a human race which had become almost universally corrupted by multiplied centuries of sellout to Satan and his cohorts. Thank God for Noah. Because of his relationship with the Creator, he became the Lord's choice to save mankind (and animals) from extinction when the universal flood blanketed the planet and forever altered its framework. Noah and his family became the ancestors of all humanity in the aftermath of that watery judgment.

The final great worldwide catastrophe to take place in Genesis is documented in the first 9 verses of chapter 11. Sadly, no righteous hero arose in the account of that disaster... only a possible villain: Nimrod (see Genesis 10:8-12). Some Bible scholars, believing his name means "we will revolt," think that Nimrod was the leader of those who in an attempt to make a name for themselves, began to build a city with "a tower that reaches to the heavens." This theory would be consistent with the fact that one of the first centers of Nimrod's kingdom was Babylon.

That name for the city where what has become known

as the "Tower of Babel" had been under construction, was the result of what God did to put a halt to the project of the people who sought to "make a name" for themselves. At that time the whole world spoke one language. That made it easy for them to work together on their insolent scheme.

Consequently the Lord created numerous other languages among them so they could no longer all communicate with each other. "Babel" likely comes from the Hebrew word for "confused." The name of the city of Babylon is derived from that same word. This historical event reminds us that when pride reaches toward the illusion of self-deification (as in the case of Lucifer), God draws the line! Despite its self-willed efforts, mankind was soon scattered over the whole earth.

The entrance of sin into this world had wrought a terrible backwash of punishments. Widespread divine tsunamis had struck the population of the planet at great cost to individuals and societies. But the Creator never totally abandoned us in spite of our prevailing wickedness. His great heart continued to long for the rich fellowship for which He'd formed man in the beginning "from the dust of the ground." Here and there in the initial trouble filled chapters of Genesis we catch glimpses of the blessings of those who pursued right relationship with the Lord. All of them found home sweet home to some degree in this life, and ultimately in its fullness for eternity.

We've briefly recounted the story of those *three* righteous men from the earliest centuries of history, but in this case they're only the lead-in to the tale of the *two* righteous men who headline the title of this book. Abraham (his later name) and Lot were both declared to have been righteous, but only one of them was honored by God with inclusion in Faith's Hall of Fame. More on the reasons for that distinction as their saga unfolds.

Their names are introduced to us in "...the account of Terah," their common ancestor. (see Genesis 11:27-32). We're told little in Scripture about Terah's life. His father was Nahor, a descendant of Noah's son, Shem. Later, in Joshua 24:2, we do learn that Terah was an idolater. We're left to speculate as to whether he eventually converted to the worship of the one true God, Yahweh, as his son, Abram, did.

Terah had lived in Ur of the Chaldeans. Chaldea was initially the name for the southern portion of Babylonia, around the lower part of the Tigris and Euphrates Rivers. Eventually, however, Chaldea came to refer to all of Babylonia. Babylonia was a pagan nation, and although the Chaldeans came to be known as the learned and wise men of the east, their intelligence was tainted with spiritual corruption, as they developed their education in a polytheistic culture. Most ancient scholars believe that the Chaldean city of Ur was located about a hundred miles southeast of the city of Babylon, on the Euphrates River.

Terah had three sons: Abram, Nahor (probably named for his grandfather), and Haran. This listing of his sons does not necessarily designate the order in which they were born. Doing some arithmetic with the ages of Terah and Abram upon Terah's death would suggest that Abram was the youngest. Haran died while the clan was still in Ur, leaving his son Lot fatherless. Abram, Lot's uncle, eventually became something of a father figure to Lot.

The names of the two women in the account, Sarai and Milcah (wives of Abram and his brother Nahor), seem to confirm that the family had been involved in idolatry.

In the Akkadian language of Chaldea, both names were connected with the Chaldean moon god. This idolatrous heritage, at least in part, was why Abram would soon be commanded by God to move on and leave his past behind him.

Before Abram's ultimate pilgrimage however, his father took him, Lot, and their families and set out for the land of Canaan (Genesis 11:31). The Bible doesn't tell us why Terah commenced this journey. Had Yahweh spoken not only to Abram, but to Terah as well, about renouncing the pagan lifestyle and going to the Promised Land? Was there some other personal reason why Terah headed westward? Or had Terah simply been accommodating his son's desire to obey God? And why did Abram's father not complete the trip, instead settling in Haran, approximately halfway to Canaan? We're left to conjecture.

One possibility that has occurred to me is that the call to establish a new nation serving the one true God may have originally rested with Terah. When he failed to carry out that calling, the mantel may have fallen upon Abram. Yet this too, is only speculation. Whatever the case, Terah died in Haran at 205 years of age, having never finished the venture. He had never even escaped the borders of Chaldea.

A notable page turns in the tale of Abram as we move from the closing verse of chapter 11 of Genesis to the opening verse of chapter 12. The patriarch of all true believers was now actually headed for home... the earthly home God Himself had ordained for him and his descendants. His step of faith came at the urging of the Almighty following Terah's passing. "The LORD had said to Abram, 'Leave your country, your people and your

father's household and go to the land I will show you'"
(Genesis 12:1).

It was effectively a world-shattering undertaking
for God's chosen servant. He was to leave his former
homeland, the citizenry he had grown up with, and his
own dear family, and travel hundreds of miles with all his
possessions and those who loved and trusted him enough
to dare to accompany him. All this was to be done without
a GPS or even a map. His destination was an unknown
area somewhere to the southwest, that God would later
show him. It took tremendous faith for Abram to obey the
call.

Not only was this man to abandon his roots, but as we
noted, he was to do so without yet knowing his destination.
Abram was instructed by God to "go to the land *I will show
you*." As he departed for this obscure territory, he had no
details on its location or characteristics.

Like the old gospel song admonishes, Abram simply
had to: "trust and obey." The life of the believer is truly a
walk of faith.

That walk is commonly revealed to us by the Lord just
one step at a time. How many of us have ever wished that
God would lay out his entire design for our lives in one
point by point document? But that's not His way of leading
us. Prove faithful in taking the first step and He'll show us
the next one. The Christian experience involves gradual
growth in the knowledge of God. Besides, if He revealed
His whole plan for our lives at once, we wouldn't be able to
handle it. We'd find out that it's too overwhelming to deal
with it all ahead of time.

This initial command from the Lord to Abram was
accompanied by the first notation of a divine covenant

tendered to the patriarch. It's this covenant relationship with Yahweh which made Abram unique in the annals of history. "I will make you into a great nation and I will bless you; I will make your name great, and you will be a blessing. I will bless those who bless you, and whoever curses you I will curse; and all peoples on earth will be blessed through you" (Genesis 12:2,3).

Notice the frequent use of several forms of the word "bless" in this covenant promise. In two sentences God uses them *five* times. Blessing is the main element of the Lord's expressed relationship with Abram. The word speaks of endowing someone with favor and happiness. God was committing Himself to blessing Abram, and blessing others through him. This is the inheritance of those who in faith decide to follow the "narrow road" that leads home to life as the Creator meant it to be (see Matthew 7:13,14).

In the years ahead, Yahweh would expand His covenant with Abram, but the basis of the first expression of it would remain intact. This alien in a strange land would *be blessed* by the Lord, and ultimately *become a blessing* to the entire population of the earth. The descendants of a once childless man would develop not only into a nation... but into a great one! The very name of their forefather would evoke respect. The benefits the covenant was to provide to others through Abram, however, were conditional. Those who blessed Abram would be blessed, while those who cursed him would be cursed. This covenant was to be broad in scope, and powerful in impact.

God had previously established a covenant following the flood of Noah's day, but it was not chiefly one of personal relationship with a single human being and his offspring. It was between the Almighty and mankind, animals, and the planet. His pledge was to never again destroy the earth with a flood. The sign of that covenant was to be the rainbow. To this day the radiant splendor of that phenomenon enchants the hearts and minds of us all whenever we see it.

But no promise of God captures the soul like that which embraces personal relationship with the Creator. This kind of covenant reflects the potential homecoming of the human race! Through God's special bond with him, Abram had become the spiritual father of all who long for that home which can only be found in the arms of the Lord.

Yet homecoming is not just a destination… it's a lifelong journey. As we strive to operate in faith and obedience to God, each new experience intensifies our understanding of Him. Day by day we can draw closer to the Lord and become more like Him. Even through painful trials and tests, our relationship with our Heavenly Father becomes the source of deep joy and satisfaction.

We tend to think of our walk with the Lord mostly as a *spiritual* pilgrimage. For Abram it touched *every area of his life*. It involved the abandonment of all that was geographically and culturally familiar. Although there was excitement over the adventure which lay ahead, there were also the fear of the unknown and the distress of losing what had been his historical identity. The man from Ur of the Chaldeans, however, would discover a new and higher identity and history in his effort to follow the leading of the Lord. The broad realities of Abram's voyage of faith have implications for our walk with God as well.

The process of getting to know the Lord is meant to grip every part of our being. As we draw closer to Jesus, His power extends into our whole existence. The impact of our journey with Him reaches to all aspects of our lives. In closing his first letter to the believers at Thessalonica, in I Thessalonians 5:23, the Apostle Paul reminded them of this vital fact. "May God himself, the God of peace, sanctify you through and through. May your *whole spirit, soul and body* be kept blameless at the coming of our Lord Jesus Christ." Nothing is to remain untouched as God sets us apart unto Himself.

Abram had to be willing to abandon much of the familiar, and welcome the new. In the natural this is no easy adjustment, but by faith he made the choice to renounce the idolatry of his native land and embrace worship of the only true God.

At what point did Abram make that pivotal decision? As we considered earlier, it may be that his father, Terah, experienced conversion, and that's why he set out for the land of promise. Abram may have in part followed his father's example. Perhaps the whole family had joined together in this newfound faith. Genesis is not clear on the matter of when, where, and how Abram became a servant of the Lord.

The early Christian martyr, Stephen, provided further insight into the timing of Abram's encounter with God. He did this during his discourse with the Sanhedrin after his arrest on false charges of blasphemy. Stephen declared: "The God of glory appeared to our father Abraham while he was still in Mesopotamia, *before* he lived in Haran. 'Leave your country and your people,' God said, 'and go to the land I will show you'" (Acts 7:2,3). This indicates that Abram's first divine calling occurred while he was still in Ur of the Chaldeans. Additionally, it informs us that it came about through a personal appearance of the God of Glory to him.

Abram was not the first to choose to return to the fellowship with the Creator for which human beings had been made. We already looked briefly at the accounts of righteous Abel, Enoch, and Noah. We also previously mentioned what Genesis 4:26 tells us, that a pre-flood movement of *corporate* devotion to God had begun. "At that time men began to call on the [personal] name of the LORD *(Yahweh, previously spelled as Jehovah)*." Unfortunately, in the centuries which ensued, mankind withdrew from that spiritual awakening to the extent that the Almighty had to destroy the entire wicked population, save Noah and his family. But now Abram commenced a revival of communion with God, one that would spread to his descendants (both physical and spiritual) for millennia to come. His story would be unique.

What of Lot, the other figure in the duo of righteous men dealt with in this book? After all, it was only to Abram that God gave the command and the covenant. We must remember though, that Lot was in the picture from the beginning of the story. Of the large group of people who must have accompanied Terah from Ur to Haran, the first leg of the journey from Chaldea to Canaan, only three were considered significant enough to mention by name: Abram, *Lot*, and Sarai (later named Sarah).

As we noted earlier, for whatever reason, Terah and his clan settled in Haran. Terah never completed the trek to the promised land. When after Terah's death Abram obeyed the Lord's directive to travel to that land, Lot joined him in that voyage of faith. The Genesis account doesn't provide detailed insights into Lot's inner thoughts on the matter, but in II Peter 2:7,8 the word "righteous" is used three times in reference to him. We know that righteousness only comes by faith, so we do know that Lot was a man of faith.

That faith had been imparted by Yahweh Himself, but we're confident that it also had been encouraged by his uncle and father figure, Abram. The pair were traveling companions on the road to home. Abram may very well have urged others in his extended family to respond to God's call and migrate with him to the land the Lord would show him. In any event, Lot was the only one to enlist with him for this lifetime of adventure. How wise it is for those who are younger to attach themselves to those who are not just *older...* but are *righteous elders* who are more mature in the faith.

The earthly home of God's chosen man and his descendants for centuries to come was their current destination. He and Lot would be tent dwellers on the way, and even after their arrival. Their ultimate destination, however, would be a metropolis of mansions on high. Abram understood this. Hebrews 11:10 says: "...he was looking forward to the city with foundations, whose architect and builder is God." Abram knew that it was only in that heavenly home that his communion with the Lord would reach its unfettered fullness. He and his family would in a sense remain pilgrims until that great eternal day when they reached Heaven.

It appears they wasted no time with distractions on the way to the land God would show Abram. The same verse which records their departure announces their arrival.

"...They set out for the land of Canaan, and they arrived there" (Genesis 12:5). Abram passed through much of that territory until he stopped at Shechem, roughly the midpoint of the region the Lord had promised to him and his people. He trusted Yahweh to fulfill His promise to make him into a "great nation" in this territory, despite the fact that it was currently plagued with a population of Canaanites with no knowledge of, or allegiance to, the one true God.

There in the midst of that heathen enclave, the Lord appeared to Abram and pledged to give the land to his offspring (Genesis12:7). This was a manifest Presence of the God of the universe to His servant. We're not told what form He took when He appeared to Abram, but based upon other such incidents in the Old Testament, the Lord may have come as an angel or even in the image of a human being. However God presented Himself, Abram responded with worship. Worship is the normal and proper response of mankind to divine manifestation. This was the first recorded incidence of the "father of the faithful" building an altar to the Lord, but by no means the last. Worship would become a lifestyle for the Lord's chosen one.

By the way, the use of that title, "father of the faithful," may have been initiated by Matthew Henry, who used it of Abraham throughout his esteemed Bible commentary. While it's not literally found in Scripture, it is consistent with descriptions of Abraham found in such passages as Romans 4:1-12 and Galatians 3:6-9.

As Abram moved further into what would become his descendants' future homeland, he again built an altar at the place where he pitched his tent between Bethel and Ai. Each altar was to be a place of worship of, and communion with, the Lord. There Abram called on the name of Yahweh. As a stranger in what was then a foreign country, he stood in demonstrative contrast to the idolatry around him. Abram was a witness to those who like him, needed to turn back to the Living God. He was walking the walk of faith.

In Genesis 12:9 we learn that Abram once more packed up his tent, and this time led his clan toward the Negev in the southern reaches of the land of promise. After what had probably seemed to be a relatively pleasant excursion so far, He likely didn't anticipate the major test of his faith which soon awaited.

Chapter 2

Abraham: Imperfect but Faithful, Part 1

(From leaving Ur of the Chaldees to the destruction of Sodom and Gomorrah)

We've established the fact that Abram and Lot were both righteous men. We're about to see, however, that they were far from perfect. This reality may initially make us disappointed in these heroes of the faith. Ultimately though, it also can be a source of encouragement to us as we struggle to overcome our own failures. This is not meant to allow us to justify or excuse our sinful shortcomings though. We must continue for a lifetime to grow in grace and strive in faith for the righteousness of God in Christ.

Let's pick up where we left off at the close of the last chapter. Perhaps to our surprise we'll discover that the first possible imperfection chronicled in the story of these men is to be seen in Abram. This is especially unexpected since this is the man whom the Bible uniquely refers to as God's *friend* (see II Chronicles 20:7, Isaiah 41:8, James 2:23).

Genesis 12:10 introduces us to Abram's first test of faith in the land of promise. The previous verse had left him headed toward the Negev. The word "Negev" (or Negeb) came to bear the double meaning of "south" or "dry," because it lay in the southern reaches of the land given to Abram and his descendants, and because it was essentially desert. Both terms have negative connotations. When we use the expression *gone south*, for instance when we say: "things have really gone south," we mean our circumstances have taken a turn for the worse. And when we as believers talk about "going through a *dry* spell," we're speaking of a difficult spiritual time when we're without any spiritual refreshment. These terms certainly describe what Abram faced in the Negev.

"Now there was a famine in the land..." (Genesis 12:10). Likely Abram wondered why God had led him into a country where it seemed he could die in such dire conditions. He wasn't the only one who could ponder whether the Lord had abandoned him in the Negev. Centuries later young David struggled with a challenging trial of his faith in that same region. Under divine command the prophet Samuel had earlier anointed David as the King of Israel. Yet before too long the one-time shepherd boy found himself repeatedly pursued in that same Negev area by an angry King Saul, bent on murdering his heir apparent. Is this how God treats His servants? How do we deal with it? How did Abram deal with it?

Scripture goes on to tell us what action Abram took. "...And Abram went down to Egypt to live there for a while because the famine was severe" (Genesis 12:10). But the account doesn't tell us what the attitude behind his action was. It does appear that he'd not permanently given up on living in the land God had shown him. Abram went to Egypt to "live there for *a while*." But was his decision to temporarily relocate, the right one or the wrong one? Was he acting in faith or unbelief? Bible scholars differ on their answers to those questions.

Some are convinced that Abram demonstrated a lack of trust in God when he headed for the ancient breadbasket of the world along the banks of the Nile River. Couldn't the Lord have *supernaturally* provided food there in the country which He had *supernaturally* consigned to Abram? They think Abram acted in unbelief and disobedience by leaving Canaan for Egypt.

Others reason that God's servant was using his divinely endowed intelligence to choose a practical solution to his dilemma. Abram didn't need to ask the Lord for a miracle when he could purchase vittles from his neighbor's overflowing storehouse. He was simply taking care of the need himself, just as most of the time we work for a living so we can buy food, rather than sitting down to an empty table and praying for our plates to be filled. This approach reminds me of something I heard spoken by a man of God many years ago. "Jesus walked on the water. Most of the time he took the boat." In other words, God uses both natural *and* supernatural means to meet our needs.

Yet another possible explanation for Abram's reaction to the problem was that he was actually following the divine plan. That's what his grandson Jacob did many years later during another famine in the promised land.

The Lord had arranged for Jacob's son Joseph to become second in command only to Pharaoh in all of Egypt. That paved the way for Jacob and the rest of the family to much later migrate southward. Not only would their stomachs be filled there, but they would experience a population explosion! Yahweh specifically told Jacob: "Do not be afraid to go down to Egypt, for I will make you into a great nation there" (Genesis 46:3).

Only God fully knows what was in Abram's heart and mind in that hour of need. One thing is sure. There in the nation of Egypt he would face yet another test of his faith. While the decision to leave Canaan for Egypt may or may not have been a righteous one, a subsequent choice made by Abram would clearly be sinful.

"As he was about to enter Egypt, he said to his wife Sarai, 'I know what a beautiful woman you are. When the Egyptians see you, they will say, 'This is his wife.' Then they will kill me but will let you live. Say you are my sister, so that I will be treated well for your sake and my life will be spared because of you'" (Genesis 12:11–13).

Abram was willing to let another man go to bed with his wife in order to save his own skin! Besides being sinful, this would also seem to be cowardly… to say nothing of indicating a lack of trust in the Lord's ability to deliver him from death. After all, God had promised to make of Abram a great nation. As yet he'd had no offspring who could become that great nation, and he'd have to remain among the living in order to produce a child. Yahweh would have to keep him alive in order to fulfill His promise.

Adultery and lying (in this case deliberately telling a misleading *half-truth* about his wife being his sister – see Genesis 20:12) are both sins. Admittedly, Abram did not yet have the Ten Commandments (which would later be given to Moses) to document that these were sins. Nonetheless, I'm sure that in his God-given conscience he knew that these were wrong. And Revelation 21:8 tells us that those who practice such sins will be cast into the lake of fire. Was this man truly the father of the faithful?

Abram certainly was right about the Egyptians recognizing Sarai's beauty. Pharaoh's officials quickly got that assessment back to him, with the result that she was brought into his palace to join the exalted ruler's harem. As Sarai's alleged brother, Abram was showered with livestock and servants for her sake. His fortune was growing, but at what price?

The Lord was about to bring this scandalous ruse to an end. Pharaoh and members of his household began to suffer serious illnesses. None of them died, however. I believe the Almighty spared their lives because Pharaoh's seemingly adulterous intentions were largely innocent since he'd been deceived about Sarai's marital status.

We're not told by what means, but the Egyptian monarch was somehow made aware that the diseases which plagued his inner circle were of divine origin. He was paying a penalty for taking another man's wife… and not just *any man's wife*. He had absconded with God's chosen servant's mate! Having gotten the message from the Almighty, Pharaoh summoned Abram to his court, chewed him out for his deception, and sent him, his wife, and everything he owned out of the country straightway. Abram avoided more severe consequences for his ill-advised actions simply because the Lord was looking out for him.

We'll skip over Genesis chapters 13 and 14 for now,

expounding on them later in chapter 4 of our book, since they deal significantly with events involving Lot. So for now we move on in the life of Abram to Genesis chapter 15, which records a fresh supernatural encounter he had with the Lord.

The first verse of Genesis 15 introduces the story: "After this, the word of the LORD came to Abram in a vision: 'Do not be afraid, Abram. I am your shield, your very great reward.'" The Hebrew word used here and translated "vision" is "machazeh." It doesn't just refer to a visible manifestation, but to one accompanied by intense pleasure. It's a vision in an ecstatic state of mind. God was not only communicating with His servant, He was doing so in an emotionally uplifting manner!

God may not often speak to us in such a dramatic fashion as He did to Abram on this occasion. Nonetheless, He's still in the business of talking to His people in various ways. The most frequent channel He uses is His written Word: the Bible. If you're not reading and studying it on a regular basis, you're greatly limiting your opportunity to hear from the Lord.

The Omnipotent One began by counseling Abram: "Do not be afraid." This is a common opening greeting from God when He speaks to His children. You'll find it throughout Scripture. The wrong kind of fear is a spiritually paralyzing agent. The enemy of our souls dispenses it wholesale in his attacks on us. Even the great patriarch was vulnerable to this devilish weapon. Indeed, we find him struggling with fear numerous times throughout his earthly pilgrimage. Fear of being killed was what had caused him to ask Sarai to lie about their being married. That fear had led to Abram's sinful behavior in Egypt.

F*ear* must first be overcome by *faith* if we're to progress in our walk with God, and Abram would need to reach out in faith to embrace the very next statement from the Lord. "I am your shield, your very great reward." Here is the foundation of faith. God not only exists, He is positively active in the experience of those who put their trust in Him. As we live in that confidence, He thwarts the schemes of Satan against us. He is our "shield."

Even better than that, the Lord is our "very great reward!" This is the essence of a relationship with God. Nothing in all the universe is as fulfilling as the bond we are designed to enjoy with our Creator. Hebrews 11:6, however, reminds us that this relationship is born of, and prospers by, the exercise of faith. "And without faith it is impossible to please God, because anyone who comes to him must believe that he exists *and* that he rewards those who earnestly seek him." Abram's *(and our)* chief reward is not a thing… it is a Person!

The patriarch's response to God's word to him in this instance began with expressions of some confusion and doubt. "But Abram said, 'O Sovereign LORD, what can you give me since I remain childless and the one who will inherit my estate is Eliezer of Damascus?' And Abram said, 'You have given me no children; so a servant in my household will be my heir'" (Genesis 15:2,3). Once again we encounter the man's spiritual imperfection.

From the human perspective we can certainly grasp Abram's perplexity… probably even identify with it. Yahweh had previously promised to make His servant into a great nation. Yet years later here he was still childless. What kind of "very great reward" was this? His apparent heir was not only from outside his family, he even hailed from outside his native land.

Questions arose as Abram pondered the situation. Had he misunderstood God's promise? Had the Lord changed His mind in the intervening years? Was the divine pledge not reliable? Every child of God has to deal with similar qualms on the road to heaven. How we deal with them is vital to our spiritual growth.

Abram placed his questions in the lap of the Almighty, and the Almighty responded quickly. That's not always the case, but this time the Lord's answer was immediate. Always be willing to wait when God's timing is not what you want. Hebrews 6:12 urges us to "...imitate those who through faith *and patience* inherit what has been promised."

While Scripture admonishes that patience be linked to our faith, it also cites patience as an attribute of God Himself. Throughout the Bible this divine characteristic is not only stated, but repeatedly demonstrated in the historical records found there. While there are limits to His patience, we clearly see that it's remarkably expansive. His kind confirmation of, and further explanation of, His promise to Abram is yet another example of it. There's no hint of anger to be found in His reaction to Abram's questioning of His purposes. We discover this same divine openness to acknowledgments of doubt and consternation often penned by the Psalmists. The Lord allows us to ask troubling questions.

God's resolution for His chosen servant's concerns was to lift his vision. Upon assuring Abram that his heir would not be a household servant as he'd supposed, but the fruit of his own loins, "He took him outside and said,

'Look up at the heavens and count the stars—if indeed you can count them.' Then he said to him, 'So shall your offspring be'" (Genesis 15:5). This amazing statement was one of the most incredible features of the Lord's destiny for Abram. It was not just the promise of a single son, but of a vast throng of descendants akin to the quantity of the countless stars in the sky above!

In that divinely ordained moment, the man's response was exactly what his Creator was desiring. "Abram believed the LORD, and he credited it to him as righteousness" (Genesis 15:6). This was the righteousness which is by faith, centuries later spoken of by the Apostle Paul throughout his New Testament epistles... the righteousness which restores relationship with God... the righteousness that sets us on the road back home! Abram had reached past his current misgivings to take God at His word and adopt a stronger, deeper faith. In spite of his shortcomings Abram was growing.

One important thing we learn from this account is that faith can grow even in the face of human apprehension. Faith ultimately overcomes doubt and fear. It's not that the child of God never doubts, it's that he or she will not allow those doubts to destroy their trust in their Heavenly Father. They press on while the enemy tries to shake their faith and block their spiritual progress. This kind of determination keeps us moving forward with God's plans even at times when it's all we can do to place one weary foot in front of another.

Immediately the Lord sought to remind Abram of His faithfulness to His servant in the past, reinforcing his faith for the future. "I am the LORD, who brought you out of Ur of the Chaldeans..." (Genesis 15:7). God also reminded him that His purpose in bringing him out of Ur to Canaan was "...to give you this land to take possession of it" (Genesis 15:7). Again, hearing a divine proclamation generated concerns in Abram's mind. "O Sovereign LORD, how can I know that I will gain possession of it?" (Genesis 15:8). Once more there's no indication that the Lord was angered by Abram's query. God looks deeper into the human heart than we can imagine, and what He saw in this man's heart beyond his obvious human frailties, was a passionate longing for his Maker.

In preparation for a fresh word to address the man's worries, God instructed Abram to prepare animal sacrifices. These offerings would be not only an act of worship on Abram's part, but the blood seal of a covenant to be made with him. Ancient covenants between parties were commonly confirmed with blood. Abram obeyed the Lord's command without hesitation and brought the sacrifices to Him. Faith and obedience are meant to go hand in hand.

Hours passed before Yahweh spoke any further. In the interim, feathered scavengers flew down and attempted to feed on the carcasses. These animal offerings belonged to God, and Abram would not allow God's property to be stolen. Each time the birds descended he drove them off. This transaction was between Abram and his Heavenly Father, and nothing would be permitted to profane this sacred moment!

"As the sun was setting, Abram fell into a deep sleep, and a thick dreadful darkness came over him" (Genesis 15:12). Though not explicitly stated, I believe the wording here indicates that this was an unnatural slumber (not simply fatigue from his extended watch over the sacrifices) induced by God in preparation for the intense spiritual experience Abram was about to undergo. The language is quite similar to that in Genesis 2:21 recounting the creation of Eve from Adam's rib: "So the LORD God caused the man to fall into a deep sleep..."

The beloved 18th century Bible commentator Matthew Henry offers helpful insight on the matter. He defines Abram's unconscious state as "...not a common sleep through weariness or carelessness, but a divine ecstasy... that, being hereby wholly taken off from the view of things sensible, he might be wholly taken up with the contemplation of things spiritual. The doors of the body were locked up, that the soul might be private and retired, and might act the more freely and like itself." In those transformational events of life that God brings our way, He may have to in essence shut down some of our natural senses in order to fully awaken our spiritual ones.

In answer to the question regarding his success in possessing the promised land, the Lord began by pulling back the curtain on a future beyond Abram's earthly sojourn. To us this appears an odd way to deal with the issue at hand. Why not start with the present, then move on to the future? It's imperative that we accept the fact that Heaven's ways are not only far above ours, but often even contrary to ours. "'For my thoughts are not your thoughts, neither are your ways my ways,' declares the LORD" (Isaiah 55:8). Our thought processes are not only limited by a finite brain, they're suffering from the corruption of sin. Trust God's Word even when you can't fully grasp it.

God informed Abram that his descendants would be enslaved in a foreign country for four centuries, but ultimately return to Canaan. Abram, however, would die in peace. The Lord also spoke of blessings upon the Israelites, and punishment upon their enemies.

Then we're told of "a smoking firepot with a blazing torch" appearing in the darkness and passing between the sacrificed animals. These items represent God's acceptance of Abram's offering and His sealing of a divine covenant with him. The Light of the World had brought light into the blackness of a man's troubled mind, and made a gracious unilateral commitment to him.

Now came the final response to Abram's query. "To your descendants I give this land..." (Genesis 15:18). Not only would Abram himself possess the fertile area Yahweh had promised, so would his children for generations to come. God had reached past his servant's weaknesses to affirm His strength and blessings upon righteous Abram and his seed.

As Genesis chapter 16 opens, we see Abram and Sarai wrestling with the fact that they still had no child to be heir to the glorious promise of God to their family. In spite of repeated words from the Lord about His plan to make Abram a great nation (and their attempts as a couple to get pregnant), Sarai was still barren.

At this season in their lives we observe once again that some questionable decisions arise. This time the choices were made not simply by Abram, but by Sarai as well, and yet a third personage entering the scene. As these determinations and their consequences are revealed, we're once more left pondering the motives and wisdom (or lack thereof) of the choices made by those involved. Was it divine direction or ancient political correctness at work?

First let's look at Sarai's initial statement on the matter

at hand. "Now Sarai, Abram's wife, had borne him no children. But she had an Egyptian maidservant named Hagar; so she said to Abram, 'The LORD has kept me from having children. Go, sleep with my maidservant; perhaps I can build a family through her'" (16:1,2). Sarai's suggestion was in keeping with the cultural norms of that time and place. Such servants were considered legal extensions of their mistresses and could become surrogate mothers. Sarai's offer to her husband was legally acceptable in this ancient land, but was it God's plan? The final answer to that question awaits us a bit later when we examine Genesis chapter 17.

The pilgrim from Ur of the Chaldees indicated that he had no major qualms about taking this course of action. "Abram agreed to what Sarai said. So after Abram had been living in Canaan 10 years, Sarai his wife, took her Egyptian maidservant Hagar and gave her to her husband to be his wife. He slept with Hagar, and she conceived" (16:2-4). Hagar had become his wife (or rather his *concubine, not a full status wife*) and was now pregnant with a child who according to the custom of the day, would be considered not only Abram's offspring, but Sarai's as well. Mission accomplished, right?

Seems it didn't take long for trouble to rear it's ugly head, though. "When she [Hagar] knew she was pregnant, she began to despise her mistress" (16:4). Pride was the original sin of Satan. Hagar sadly fell under that same spell. She was also acting against one of the Lord's basic principles of respect for authority when she treated her mistress rudely.

Sarai then soon turned on her husband, Abram. The very next verse (16:5) declares that she charged *him* with this alleged crime. "You are responsible for the wrong I am suffering. I put my servant in your arms, and now that she knows she is pregnant, she despises me. May the LORD judge between you and me." I wonder how often you and I may have been instrumental in creating a mess, and then blamed it on someone else? Methinks Sarai was neither the first or the last to cheat while playing the blame game.

The head of the house reacted by affording Sarai the authority to take whatever acts of retribution she desired upon Hagar. "'Your servant is in your hands,' Abram said. 'Do with her whatever you think best.' Then Sarai mistreated Hagar; so she fled from her" (16:6). This is clearly not the kind of attitude God wants His people to have toward those who are unkind to us. In Luke 6:27,28 Jesus instructed His followers to "...do good to those who hate you, bless those who curse you, pray for those who mistreat you."

The negative attitudes and actions which quickly became byproducts of Sarai's solution to the problem of her barrenness, are easily seen as evidence of the lack of any divine endorsement of her plan. How readily we open the windows of our souls to turbulent winds when, in doubt, frustration, or impatience, we develop our own schemes for achieving God's will. The Lord needs our cooperation, but not our advice.

The Almighty may not have fully approved of the means Sarai and Abram used to seek the fulfillment of His promises to bless Abram's descendants, but He was not about to punish Hagar and her unborn child for those actions, nor even for Hagar's own subsequent arrogance toward her mistress. Our merciful Savior pursued her in her flight, and found her near a desert spring, apparently on her way back to her native Egypt. It's interesting to note that He greeted her as the "servant of Sarai..." *not* as the wife of Abram.

God knew what she was doing, where she was headed, and why. Still, He asked her what was going on, allowing Hagar herself to confess. After she admitted what was happening, the Lord pointed her in a different direction. "Go back to your mistress and submit to her," (16:9) the angel of the Lord instructed the runaway servant.

This command was not without a powerful word of promise to encourage her on her way. He added, "I will so increase your descendants that they will be too numerous to count" (16:10). He went on to foretell some details of her son's future and that of his offspring. God also gave him a name indicative of how He'd dealt with Hagar in her time of distress. "Ishmael" means "God hears." In turn, she gave the Lord a name. "Beer Lahai Roi," which translates as "well of the Living One who sees me." The fountain nearby was called by that very title for centuries to come.

This episode demonstrated that although Ishmael was not to be the son of Yahweh's unique covenant with Abram, he was nonetheless loved by God. I also deem it significant that the angel of the LORD did not tell Hagar that her womb now contained *fetal tissue*. He clearly declared: "You are now with *child*..." (16:11). And God had a plan for that child's life. May we value the unborn as much as our Creator.

A short time later Abram became a father for the first time at the age of 86. According to the word of the Lord, he named his firstborn Ishmael.

Abram's next encounter with God (recorded in Genesis chapter 17) confirms the fact that the course of action proposed by Sarai and carried out by Abram and Hagar, was not part of the covenant plan the Lord had initiated for the blessing of the patriarch's progeny. In fact, in Galatians 4:21-31 the Apostle Paul demonstrates how the *Hagar solution* to the problem of Sarai's barrenness represents the works-based efforts of the flesh nature to accomplish the fulfillment of a divine promise which can really only be accomplished by the Spirit of God in response to our faith!

13 years had passed since the birth of Ishmael when the Lord appeared before Abram to further define His covenant. It behooves us to remember that God often reveals His plans for our own lives a portion at a time over the course of our spiritual journey, just as he did with Abram.

In this instance the Lord introduced Himself as "God Almighty." In the original Hebrew this is the compound word "El-Shaddai." While it appears a number of times throughout the Old Testament, this occasion is the very first time that particular divine title is used in Scripture. "El" is the short version of the term "Elohim," which simply means "God." There is much more to be understood about this word, but for the moment our emphasis is on the second half of the compound: "Shaddai."

As it is here in Genesis 17:1, "Shaddai" is generally rendered "Almighty" in English translations of the Bible, but the meaning is deeper and fuller than that. In his late nineteenth century work: "Synonyms of the Old Testament," the former principal of Wycliffe Hall, Oxford, England, Robert B. Girdlestone, defines it as follows:

"The title **Shaddai** really indicates the fullness and riches of God's grace, and would remind the Hebrew reader that from God cometh every good and perfect gift;—that

He is never weary of pouring forth His mercies upon His people, and that he is more ready to give than they are to receive. ...Perhaps the expressive word bountiful would convey the sense most exactly. This rendering will be illustrated and confirmed by a reference to some of the passages in which **Shaddai** occurs, as they will be found specially to designate God as a Bountiful Giver."

This understanding of El-Shaddai will help us grasp the nature of God's covenant with Abram and the subsequent requirements thrust upon the man and his descendants. The first of those obligations is stated in the latter half of 17:1: "...walk before me and be *blameless.*" Wow! The King James Version translation of the final word of this phrase is perhaps even more intimidating: "perfect!"

We've already established that to this point in his experience Abram was certainly not perfect in the absolute sense in which we normally view the term. Would he from this moment on become perfect or blameless? How about King David? Was he perfect? In Psalm 26:1 David used the same Hebrew root to ask God Himself to vindicate him, proclaiming "...for I have led a blameless life..."

Surely we need a greater understanding of the word blameless in this passage. Otherwise, along with Abram we'll find ourselves facing a humanly impossible task. We must begin by reminding ourselves that the Lord began this discussion with His servant by referring to Himself as El-Shaddai; Shaddai indicating "the fullness and riches of God's grace!"

Now let's take a closer look at the Hebrew word "tāmîm," here translated as "perfect" or "blameless." It's an adjective, with a definition not restricted only to *perfect or blameless*... but alternately meaning *sincerity, entire, whole, complete, or full*. It can refer to someone or something simply being whole or intact, not broken up or divided. This broadens our comprehension of the term beyond the narrow perception of totally unblemished perfection.

"Nelson's Expository Dictionary of the Old Testament" sheds a revealing light on its use in the text we're currently examining:

> "In Judges 9:16, where tāmîm describes a relationship between men it is clear that more than mere external activity is meant: 'Now therefore, if ye have done truly and sincerely [literally, "in a sincere manner"], in that ye have made Abimelech king...' This extended connotation of this nuance is also evidenced when one compares Genesis 17:1 with Rom. 4 where Paul argues that Abraham fulfilled God's condition but that he did so only through faith."

The above cited 4th chapter of Romans assures us that Abram's righteousness (blamelessness, perfection, sincerity, wholeness, completeness, fullness) came not by his own works (good deeds, laudable actions, etc.), but *only by faith through grace*. That righteousness by faith was bestowed upon him years earlier when he accepted the truth of God's covenant promises given to him in chapter 15. "Abram believed the LORD, and he credited it to him as righteousness" (Genesis 15:6).

In telling Abram to "...walk before me and be blameless,"

He was urging His friend to *maintain* the walk of faith by grace. That was the basis of his relationship with the Lord. God then declared that the result would be that "I will confirm my covenant between me and you and will greatly increase your numbers" (17:2). Abram fell face down in worship before Yahweh, and in the following 11 verses God elaborated further on the covenant.

"You will be the father of many nations" (17:4). Romans 4:16,17 explains what that means. "Therefore, the promise comes by faith, so that it may be by grace and may be guaranteed to all Abraham's offspring—not only to those who are of the law but also to those who are of the faith of Abraham. He is the father of us all. As it is written: 'I have made you a father of many nations.' He is our father in the sight of God, in whom he believed—the God who gives life to the dead and calls things that are not as though they were." As we mentioned earlier, Abraham is called "the father of the faithful." That term "faithful" applies not only to *Jews* who believe, but to those of any and every nation who place their faith in Christ. Thus Abraham is the father *of many nations.*

A name change coincided with this promise of God. "No longer will you be called Abram; your name will be Abraham, for I have made you a father of many nations" (17:5). Abram means *exalted father.* Abraham means *father of many.* A man to whom the Lord had already promised offspring as numerous as the stars of heaven (Genesis 15:5), was now to be made even more fruitful. Nations and kings would come from him! (17:6).

God's covenant with Abraham would extend to all of his descendants forever. The Lord would always be his God and their God. Abraham's natural offspring were to be given the entire land of Canaan as their own permanent property. A divine condition was placed upon the fulfillment of these promises. All involved had to *keep the principles of the covenant* (see 17:7-9).

A physical token of this covenant was then established by God. "Every male among you shall be circumcised. You are to undergo circumcision, and it will be the sign of the covenant between me and you" (17:10,11). Circumcision was primarily to be performed at the age of 8 days upon every male child born to Abraham and his offspring. But the rite was to be extended to any male of any age, even all those of Abraham's household who were not his descendants. This meant that everyone who committed themselves to the Abrahamic Covenant with Yahweh in this manner became members of that covenant. This foreshadowed the wholesale extension of the New Covenant to *all* people. "For God so loved *the world...*" (John 3:16).

Why circumcision? There is no direct rationale given in Scripture. As with many of God's later commands to His chosen people, research data has shown that circumcision appears to have physical health benefits. But the primary rationale for it would seem to be spiritual symbolism. My personal speculation is that the removal of the foreskin, which might be considered a potential impediment to marital intimacy, represents the Lord's desire for unencumbered spiritual intimacy with mankind.

This higher representation can be seen in Paul's discussion in Romans 2:28,29 of how the New Covenant supersedes the Old Covenant. "A man is not a Jew if he is only one outwardly, nor is circumcision merely outward and physical. No, a man is a Jew if he is one inwardly; and circumcision is circumcision of the heart, by the Spirit, not by the written code. Such a man's praise is not from men, but from God." The *physical* circumcision of the foreskin as a sign of the Abrahamic Covenant, paralleled the *spiritual* circumcision of the *heart* under the New Covenant.

Abraham's obedience to the Lord's command of the rite of circumcision was immediate. "On that very day Abraham took his son Ishmael and all those born in his household or bought with his money, and circumcised them, as God told him" (17:23). Unless He specifically directs us to a future schedule as such, the best thing we can do when God instructs us on any matter is to act on that command at our first opportunity. Otherwise, delay invites hindrances.

After dealing with the issue of *all the me*n in his household, God turned the conversation to the *one woman* of most import in his life: Sarai. Another name change in the family, and the reason behind that name change, was revealed by the Sovereign of the Universe. "God also said to Abraham, 'As for Sarai your wife, you are no longer to call her Sarai; her name will be Sarah. I will bless her and will surely give you a son by her. I will bless her so that she will be the mother of nations; kings of peoples will come from her'" (17:15,16). It's not clear what the meaning of her original name was, but the new version speaks of her divine promotion. Sarah means "princess."

Abraham's instant reaction to this word of the Lord was anything but commendable. As he did earlier in this third encounter with the Almighty, he again fell face down. Before, his prostrate posture was an appropriate response of humble worship. This time his demeanor would seem to be one of hilarious disbelief! "...He laughed and said to himself, 'Will a son be born to a man a hundred years old? Will Sarah bear a child at the age of ninety?'" (17:17).

In his incredulity Abraham offered a better *(humanly speaking)* suggestion for the Lord. "And Abraham said to God, 'If only Ishmael might live under your blessing!'" (17:18) This request may have stemmed from a father's love for his firstborn, but it missed the mark. God had a higher plan. He reiterated His intention to supernaturally give Abraham and Sarah a son of their own. He declared that the everlasting covenant would flow through that son and his descendants. The Lord even gave that child a name in advance, one which would remind Abraham that God can and will do the miraculous even when His servant thinks the idea is laughable. The name Isaac means "he laughs."

The fact that God had foreordained that the Abrahamic Covenant would flow through a life conceived by Abraham and Sarah rather than one produced by Abram and Hagar, doesn't mean the Lord didn't care about Ishmael. When Abraham asked God to bless Ishmael, the very next word from the mouth of the Lord was: "Yes" (17:19). After reaffirming His plans for Isaac, God went on to pronounce His good intentions toward Abram's firstborn. "And as for Ishmael, I have heard you: I will surely bless him; I will make him fruitful and will greatly increase his numbers, He will be the father of twelve rulers, and I will make him into a great nation" (17:20).

The Lord then informed Abraham that Sarah would give birth to Isaac "by this time next year" (17:21). Having established the schedule for the fulfillment of the promise, Yahweh returned to His throne in heaven.

Sometime in the near future God returned to visit His

human friend once again, although this time the Lord did not initially reveal His identity. Neither did Abraham at first recognize the divine nature of one of his guests. The 1st verse of Genesis chapter 18 sets the scene as "near the great trees of Mamre," the area where Abraham first set up camp years earlier after returning from Egypt. The soon to be host was attempting to keep cool in the heat of the day by relaxing in the shade under the opening of his tent.

The Lord was apparently accompanied by two of His angels, although Abraham saw all three simply as men. He rushed to meet them and bowed in deference. "He said, 'If I have found favor in your eyes, my lord, do not pass your servant by. Let a little water be brought, and then you may all wash your feet and rest under this tree. Let me get you something to eat, so you can be refreshed and then go on your way—now that you have come to your servant'" (18:3-5).

Some advice found in Hebrews 13:2 quickly comes to mind. "Do not forget to entertain strangers, for by so doing some people have entertained angels without knowing it." In this instance Abraham was not just providing hospitality for two angels, but also to the Almighty Himself!

When his guests consented, Abraham quickly set Sarah to work preparing a hearty meal. It took some time to get this extensive lunch together, including the slaughter and butchering of a choice calf. By the time it was served, the sun had perhaps descended enough to allow them to comfortably dine in the open. Out of respect, Abraham did not enjoy the food with them, but stood under a nearby tree as a humble waiter.

Soon the Lord got to the primary purpose of the visit.

Once more the message from heaven concerned the as yet unborn heir of the covenant. "'Where is your wife Sarah?' they asked him. 'There, in the tent,' he said" (18:6). God went on to reaffirm to Abraham His plan for Sarah to have that son of promise just a year from now. On this occasion, however, Abraham's ears were not the only ones to tune in to such astounding news. Sarah herself was eavesdropping at the entrance to the tent. Evidently Abraham had not shared with his wife this word from the Lord previously given to him.

She was well aware of how absurd such a proposal was. The couple were both old, and in particular she'd been barren her whole life, and even if she had been fertile she was now beyond the age when becoming pregnant was a possibility. Just imagining this scenario generated a silent chuckle. Her giggle may not have been audible to human ears, but nothing is hidden for the Creator of the universe.

"Then the LORD said to Abraham, 'Why did Sarah laugh and say, "Will I really have a child, now that I am old?" Is anything too hard for the LORD? I will return to you at the appointed time next year and Sarah will have a son'" (18:13,14). Fearful and likely embarrassed, she denied laughing. But God is never fooled by our lies.

Husband and wife had both been plainly given the promise of the miraculous conception and birth of their son, and both had initially reacted with laughter stemming from some level of unbelief. Yet God's precious pledge had not been withdrawn. Faith was growing where doubt had been, and in another flip of the calendar Isaac would be born. The seed of faith would overcome human frailty.

And yes, as previously mentioned, Abraham ultimately did come to be known as the "father of the faithful."

The first mention of the two wicked cities of Sodom and Gomorrah is in Genesis 13:10. When Abram and Lot were forced to separate, Lot chose to relocate to that area. In chapter 4 of this book we'll examine Lot's involvement in that neighborhood in more detail. But in this 18th chapter of Genesis we're introduced to the pending destruction of these two towns.

Genesis 18:16 tells us that the Lord had finished His dialogue with Abraham and Sarah on the issue of the coming birth of Isaac, and He and His angelic companions prepared to depart. The heavenly trio headed down toward Sodom, and Abraham courteously chose to walk with them for some distance, to see his guests on their way.

Beginning at verse 17, the Bible records an interesting conversation carried on by God. Was He talking simply to Himself, to His angels, or to Abraham? We're not told. However, it seems possible that verses 17 through 19 were His own private musings, while verses 20 and 21 were spoken aloud to Abraham. Whatever the case, the subject the Lord speaks about at this point is distinctly different from that of the discourse he engaged in back at the tent.

"Then the LORD said, 'Shall I hide from Abraham what I am about to do? Abraham will surely become a great and powerful nation, and all nations on earth will be blessed through him. For I have chosen him, so that he will direct his children and his household after him to keep the way of the LORD by doing what is right and just, so that the LORD will bring about for Abraham what he has promised him.' Then the LORD said, 'The outcry against Sodom and Gomorrah is so great and their sin so grievous that I will go down and see if what they have done is as bad as the outcry that has reached me. If not, I will know'" (18:17-21).

Then the two angels left the Lord and Abraham behind and continued the journey to Sodom. Before we move on to the ensuing discussion about Sodom and Gomorrah between God and His servant, let's make a couple of observations about the things God said in the above quoted passage.

Yahweh determined not to withhold from Abraham his plans for dealing with the two wicked cities. His reason for divulging such momentous plans to His earthly servant have to do with the calling and covenant relationship that rested upon this single individual. Not only would Abraham's own descendants become a great nation, but through this man the heavenly blessings would extend to *all* nations! God's plan included Abraham's preeminent seed, Jesus, becoming the Savior of *the world* centuries later.

Abraham's assignment was not simply to charge his genetic offspring, but also all others under his roof, to maintain godly lifestyles. Though the Israelites would become God's *chosen people*, the ultimate objective of Abraham's testimony through the ages was to make God's goodness available to the whole planet. The personal commitment to, and propagation of, righteousness by faith would enable the fulfillment of all the promises of the Abrahamic covenant.

Such expansive outgrowth of personal faith in God is not meant to be a product of Abraham's life alone, but of every believer's life. The Lord's intention is not only to bless us, but to extend His blessing to others through us. We're all called to share the good news that through faith every willing human being can be reconciled to the loving God from whom we were alienated because of sin. This glorious truth applied even to the inhabitants of Sodom and Gomorrah.

I believe that in the statements about Abraham in this context, the Lord was not just summing up his responsibilities, but was expressing confidence in the man's faithfulness to carry out those responsibilities. This is evidenced by the fact that God prefaced His remarks about Abraham's future destiny with the word "*surely.*" Then He reinforced His confidence in the man's character by noting: "For I have chosen him, so that *he will...*" God's declarations were a divine endorsement of His faithful servant! May we all seek to live so that we may one day hear our Heavenly Father declare: "Well done, good and faithful servant!"

It was important that God's friend experience a growing understanding of the ways of the Lord. Abraham's ongoing pursuit of a deeper relationship with the Almighty qualified him for such greater spiritual revelations. This is one of the blessings given to those who follow God closely.

God shared with Abraham His concerns over the gross sinfulness of Sodom and Gomorrah. He explained that there had been a great outcry over their debauchery. Traditionally, an outcry in Scripture arises from those who are being oppressed. While Sodom is primarily notorious for its perverse sexual sins, there are other evils noted as part of their wickedness. In Ezekiel 16:49,50 God cites other trespasses. "Now this was the sin of... Sodom: She and her daughters were arrogant, overfed and unconcerned; they did not help the poor and needy. They were haughty and did detestable things before me. Therefore I did away with them as you have seen." It appears these people were also arrogant, glutenous, selfish, and heartless.

The Just Ruler of Heaven and Earth could not ignore wickedness so severe that it reached beyond its borders to harshly mistreat helpless neighbors. He had to do something about it. He determined to "go down and see" exactly how bad it was.

It's necessary at this juncture to remember that God is omniscient. That is, He knows *everything*. He didn't need to visit the planet to discover all the details for Himself. I'm convinced that what He said in this passage is largely metaphoric. He went down to demonstrate that unlike human beings He doesn't act on rumor alone. The Lord always acts on the facts, and cares enough about the inhabitants of earth to come down to their level.

Additionally, in the midst of this situation He arrived to present His servant with an opportunity to get involved. During the discussion that begins in 18:23 we witness a vital spiritual ministry carried out by Abraham... a ministry which is a high calling entered into by God's dearest saints: intercession. Intercession is intense prayer for others, especially those in danger of judgment for sin at the hands of a holy God. By interceding we entreat the Lord to show mercy. We can become a conduit of His grace. God seeks such servants.

Prophets (God proclaimed Abraham a prophet in Genesis 20:7) speak out to people to warn of potential punishment, urging them to repent. But they also petition God in a further effort to stave off judgment. This ministry is consistent with the heart of the Almighty. II Peter 3:9 tells us "The Lord is not slow in keeping his promise, as some understand slowness. He is patient with you, not wanting anyone to perish, but everyone to come to repentance."

Sadly though, sometimes when He searches for just such an intercessor, He finds no one willing. This was the situation on one occasion when the people of Israel had rebelled against Yahweh, committing all kinds of grievous sins. Following a failed recruitment effort, God lamented the lack of a volunteer to pray. "I looked for a man among them who would build up the wall and stand before me in the gap on behalf of the land so I would not have to destroy it, but I found none" (Ezekiel 22:30).

Thankfully, at other times He found a man or woman with a heart for God and humanity. There are a number of examples cited in the Bible, but two come to mind most readily.

Moses was such a leader. On their way to the promised land, the Israelites forsook the Lord, creating a golden calf to worship. Then they indulged in what many Bible scholars believe was a mass drunken sex orgy. About three-thousand people lost their lives that day as a result of their sin, but the majority found mercy in answer to Moses' heartfelt intercession. You can read the story in Exodus chapter 32.

The highest model of an intercessor, however, is unquestionably the Lord Jesus Christ Himself. Shortly before His sacrificial death for all who would believe, He poured out His heart in loving intercession to the Father. In John chapter 17 we find Jesus praying intensely for the Father to watch over His disciples and all who would choose to follow Him in all the centuries to come, ultimately bringing them to heaven to spend eternity with Him. And on the cross we hear Him intercede for the sinners who abused and murdered Him. "...Father, forgive them, for they do not know what they are doing" (Luke 23:34).

We first gained a glimpse of Abraham engaging in a measure of this ministry of intercession in Genesis 17:18 when he pleaded with the Lord for divine blessing upon Ishmael. This time, however, the man prayed not for his own son, but for the citizens of Sodom and Gomorrah... particularly Sodom. Perhaps the focus was more heavily upon Sodom because that's where Abraham's nephew Lot and his family were living. Or perhaps because Sodom may have been the original cauldron where the recipe for the region's sinful debauchery was stewed.

Abraham approached the Lord and began by appealing to God's impeccable sense of justice. "Will you sweep away the righteous with the wicked? What if there are fifty righteous people in the city? Will you really sweep it away and not spare the place for the sake of the fifty righteous people in it? Far be it from you to do such a thing—to kill the righteous with the wicked, treating the righteous and the wicked alike. Far be it from you! Will not the Judge of all the earth do right?" (18:23-25).

The divine response was exactly what Abraham was hoping for when he presented God with that potential moral dilemma. "The LORD said, 'If I find fifty righteous people in the city of Sodom, I will spare the whole place for their sake'" (18:26). The scenario Yahweh's friend outlined was simply an opportunity for God to demonstrate the vast dimensions of His merciful nature.

But Abraham the intercessor was not finished. He

knew he'd been presumptuous to speak so daringly to the Judge of the whole earth, and consequently acknowledged it, yet pressed on in the legal argument as he saw it. "Then Abraham spoke up again: 'Now that I have been so bold as to speak to the Lord, though I am nothing but dust and ashes, what if the number of the righteous is five less than fifty? Will you destroy the whole city because of five people?'" (18:27,28).

On and on he went, repeatedly reducing the possible number of godly citizens living in Sodom, pressing God to reduce the size of His requirements for sparing that whole community filled with wicked sinners. Over and over a loving Lord committed to hold back His wrath as the numbers grew vastly smaller.

Finally Abraham's challenge to God's merciful nature drew to a close. "Then he said, 'May the Lord not be angry, but let me speak just once more. What if only ten can be found there?' He answered, 'For the sake of ten, I will not destroy it'" (18:32). The two parted company, Abraham having fulfilled his calling as an intercessor. What was the end result of this divine/human interaction concerning the fate of the two wicked cities? Genesis chapter 19 provides the answer to that question, and deals largely with Lot. So we'll discuss that in chapter 4 of our book.

Chapter 3

Abraham: Imperfect but Faithful, Part 2

(From the Abimelech crisis to the death of Abraham)

It's been said that history repeats itself. When good history is repeated, that's beneficial; but when bad history is repeated it's detrimental. Genesis chapter 20 chronicles an instance of the latter in the life of Abraham. Once more we're confronted with the patriarch's imperfections.

Abraham decided to move on in his sojourning through the land God had pledged to him and his posterity. He left Mamre and headed for a region where he'd stayed years earlier: the Negev. This time he settled between Kadesh and Shur, living for a while in the Philistine town of Gerar. It was there where he in essence repeated some bad personal history.

Remember when earlier in Egypt Abraham and Sarah (as directed by her husband) together propagated the misleading half-truth that they were actually just brother and sister rather than husband and wife? In so doing the man of God opened the door for adultery, in an unholy effort to save his own skin. Only by the grace of God was Pharaoh kept from committing adultery with Sarah.

In an encore at Gerar, Abraham again chose to practice deception rather than trust God to protect him. Fear was allowed to overcome faith. Personal misconduct triumphed over godly integrity... and this was not the first time! Further, later in this story we'll discover that this practice had been *habitual!*

The latent adulterous man in this case was not Egypt's Pharaoh, but Gerar's Philistine king: Abimelech. Under false pretenses created by the Lord's servant himself, the king took Sarah into his harem. This time Abraham's misdeed was even more grievous than before, in view of the fact that God had recently revealed to him that Sarah would become pregnant by him and become the mother of the child of the covenant. It appears Abraham was willing to risk his wife becoming pregnant by another man. Fortunately, Yahweh would intervene once more to prevent a bad situation from escalating into a much worse one.

Thank God that He often steps in to help when we are weak and sinful. The Savior was not approving Abraham's bad behavior. He wasn't even excusing it. The Lord was acting on the man's behalf because he was His friend. God's intervention was not an endorsement of Abraham's sin, it was an endorsement of their precious covenant relationship. We witness instances of this type of divine mediation throughout God's Word.

Under the New Covenant God's Son has now taken

on the role of mediator. In this capacity He serves as the primary link between sinful humanity and a holy God. I Timothy 2:5 says: "For there is one God and one mediator between God and men, the man Christ Jesus..." As New Testament believers we have a holy advocate who steps in to aid us in our own weak and disobedient actions, as were Abraham's in this instance. This is not provided to excuse our sins or to encourage us to continue in them, but to offer forgiveness and foster a desire to move forward and grow in the faith. "My dear children, I write this to you so that you will not sin. But if anybody does sin, we have one who speaks to the Father in our defense—Jesus Christ, the Righteous One" (I John 2:1).

In the midst of Abraham's self-made dilemma, *good* history was now about to repeat itself. It may not have seemed good to Abimelech though, when God first appeared to him in a dream. The Almighty declared: "You are as good as dead because of the woman you have taken; she is a married woman" (20:3).

Immediately recognizing that this was no normal dream, Abimelech began to plead with the one true God. Knowing he had not consummated his sexual desires with Sarah, and that he was ignorant of her true marital status, he asserted his personal innocence, and consequently that of the nation he ruled. Both Abraham and Sarah had disclosed to Abimelech only a misleading exaggeration of their relationship as step-siblings.

Yahweh agreed with the king's assertion. "Then God said to him in the dream, 'Yes, I know you did this with a clear conscience, and so I have kept you from sinning against me'" (20:6). The Lord went on to tell Abimelech that it was He who kept the king from sinning because of the monarch's innocence in the matter. The question then arises: why did God tell the man that he was as good as dead?

In my estimation the answer is two-fold. First, *God the Judge* wanted Abimelech to be fully aware of the gravity of the sin which lay just behind the door the Almighty had to this point compassionately kept closed. In the Lord's book it would have been a capital crime. Secondly, *God the Savior* wanted him to know that He is merciful, and that in His compassion He had prevented this pagan ruler from crossing that fatal threshold.

Directing Abimelech into the path of repentance, the Lord instructed him to reverse course. "Now return the man's wife, for he is a prophet, and he will pray for you and you will live. But if you do not return her, you may be sure that you and all yours will die" (20:7). God's plan is that *conviction of sin* is to be followed by *repentance from sin*. That's how we move from a sinful lifestyle to a godly one.

There was little hesitation on the part of Abimelech. The next morning he gathered his officials and shared the bad news/good news message from his encounter with God the night before. He understood that this situation would affect not only him, but his entire realm. The reaction of those in his governing cabinet was fear. Thankfully, the king's next step would remove the risk of divine condemnation currently hanging over their collective heads.

In obedience to the Lord's command, Abimelech returned Sarah to Abraham, but not without first justifiably chiding Abraham for his contribution to the crisis at hand. "Then Abimelech called Abraham in and said, 'What have you done to us? How have I wronged you that you have brought such great guilt upon me and my kingdom? You have done things to me that should not be done.' And Abimelech asked Abraham, 'What was your reason for doing this?'" (20:9,10). Now it was Abraham's turn to deal with conviction. In some ways he was more at fault than Abimelech. It was probably because of his overall faithfulness to God that the Lord's grace covered him in this affair.

Abraham's confession to Abimelech is recorded in verses 11-13. "...I said to myself, 'There is surely no fear of God in this place, and they will kill me because of my wife.' Besides, she really is my sister, the daughter of my father though not of my mother; and she became my wife. And when God had me wander from my father's household, I said to her, 'This is how you can show your love to me: Everywhere we go, say of me, He is my brother.'"

This is where we discover that Abraham's propagation of this deceitful half-truth had been his pattern for all the years since his departure from Ur of the Chaldees. The predicament faced by him in Gerar was the second of it's kind found in the Bible; the first being the situation in Egypt involving Pharaoh. However, Abraham's carnal and fearful behavior had been habitually practiced by him and Sarah for decades.

Ironically, Abraham's son of promise later repeated his father's same spiritual blunder. In Genesis chapter 26 we can read how Isaac told Abimelech (either the very same king or perhaps his son, heir to the throne, and namesake) that his wife (and cousin) Rebekah was his sister. Although Isaac's folly didn't result in the king taking Rebekah into his harem, it did risk that potential consequence. Parents, we're reminded that our children may not only follow our good examples, but our bad ones as well… even ones they have not actually seen.

Upon hearing Abraham's candid explanation, Abimelech returned Sarah to him, along with gifts of livestock and slaves to make amends for taking her in the first place. Unlike Pharaoh, the monarch of Gerar did not drive Abraham out of his realm. Instead, he generously said, "My land is before you; live wherever you like" (20:15).

Abimelech then turned to address the wife he'd just restored to Abraham. "To Sarah he said, 'I am giving your brother a thousand shekels of silver. This is to cover the offense against you before all who are with you; you are completely vindicated'" (20:16). This was a gesture in compensation for the disgrace he'd brought upon her and her husband by seizing Sarah with the intent of making her his mistress, and then consigning her to his harem.

In the opening statement of verse 17 we find Abraham praying for Abimelech just as the Lord had promised in the king's dream the night before. Chapter 20 then closes out the story with God's answer to that prayer, revealing a previously undisclosed consequence of the king's sin. "…and God healed Abimelech, his wife and his slave girls so they could have children again, for the LORD had closed up every womb in Abimelech's household because of Abraham's wife Sarah." So we view yet another demonstration of both God's justice and His mercy.

As Genesis chapter 21 begins, we learn that after the opening of the wombs of all the women in Abimelech's household, the Lord soon also opened Sarah's womb, just as He had promised earlier. The subject of her pregnancy is introduced with a key word. "Now the LORD was *gracious* to Sarah…" (21:1). Grace was certainly needed because when God had first promised her a child, she doubted. Still, it's critical that we as believers always remember that even when we're honoring God by acting in faith and obedience, every blessing which comes our way flows only through *His grace!*

Certainly the greatest blessing of all is undeserved. "For it is by grace you have been saved, through faith— and this not from yourselves, it is the gift of God— not by works, so that no one can boast. For we are God's workmanship, created in Christ Jesus to do good works, which God prepared in advance for us to do" (Ephesians 2:8-10).

The promised conception and birth may have arrived late in the estimation of Abraham and Sarah (him at age 100 and her at age 90), but in God's determination things were right on time. Scripture declares that the events occurred "...at the very time God had promised him" (21:2). Sometimes, as in this case of the birth of the son of promise, the Sovereign One provides us with His schedule in advance. Most of the time, however, we must press on while trusting the wisdom of His timing. Like David we ought to be able to say in retrospect: "I waited patiently for the LORD..." (Psalm 40:1).

According to God's command in Genesis 17:19, Abraham named his son, "Isaac," meaning "he laughs." Both the boy's father and mother had laughed in reaction to Yahweh's proclamation that they would have a child in their old age. Their initial snickering was an expression of disbelief at the ridiculous idea that with one foot in the grave, they could before long be actually placing an infant in a cradle!

Now Sarah's laughter came from a different

perspective. It was a pleasant expression of amazement at the miracle the Lord Himself had performed on their behalf, for their benefit and His glory. "Sarah said, 'God has brought me laughter, and everyone who hears about this will laugh with me.' And she added, 'Who would have said to Abraham that Sarah would nurse children? Yet I have borne him a son in his old age'" (21:6,7).

Right on schedule the covenant son was marked with the sign of the covenant by his father. "When his son Isaac was eight days old, Abraham circumcised him, as God commanded him" (21:4). Despite his numerous imperfections, this frequent pattern of ultimate obedience to the Lord's requirements has come to reflect why this man was considered faithful by his Maker.

A few years later, on the very day Isaac was weaned, Abraham threw a great celebration. Unfortunately, this feast was to be spoiled by troubling events. In front of Sarah and other celebrants, Ishmael, who would have then probably been in his teens, began mocking his younger half-brother. Sarah's wrath had been stirred years before when, while pregnant with Ishmael, Hagar had begun to despise her mistress. This time it was Hagar's son who disrespected Sarah's son.

Sarah had had enough! In anger she demanded that her husband cut ties completely with the offensive pair. "...And she said to Abraham, 'Get rid of that slave woman and her son, for that slave woman's son will never share in the inheritance with my son Isaac'" (21:10). You may recall that Hagar's son was originally meant to be considered Sarah's child. Hagar was to have been a surrogate mother for Sarah. Now Sarah not only failed to recognize Ishmael in that manner, she wouldn't even use his name. She referred to him as "that slave woman's son."

Furthermore, Sarah did not even acknowledge that Ishmael was her husband's own son... born of a strategy for addressing their childlessness suggested by Sarah herself! This chapter began by noting that God had been gracious to Sarah. Should she not have been gracious to Ishmael and Hagar... and to Ishmael's father, Abraham? He was in anguish over the situation. In spite of the palpably heartless nature of his wife's angry demand; however, God gave it the green light.

"...Do not be so distressed about the boy and your maidservant. Listen to whatever Sarah tells you, because it is through Isaac that your offspring will be reckoned. I will make the son of the maidservant into a nation also, because he is your offspring" (21:12,13). Perhaps somewhat comforted by this word from the Lord, Abraham obeyed God. The very next morning he provided Hagar with food and water and sent her and Ishmael away. It's not always easy to walk in faith and obedience, but it's fundamental to becoming a faithful servant of the Lord.

Hagar evidently headed out in the general direction of her native Egypt. Yet seeming to have no clear bearings, she and her son wandered in the desert of Beersheba. Eventually they ran out of water. In despair she settled her son in the shade of some bushes and sat down some distance away, unable to bear the thought of watching him die. Overwhelmed by hopelessness, Hagar sobbed and Ishmael cried.

Just as God had intervened years earlier when Hagar and her then unborn son had fled to the desert, so He would not leave them abandoned this time either. Nothing in His universe escapes the Lord's notice. While God does not approve of bad behavior, He nonetheless loves all who who are guilty of it. Yahweh heard Ishmael crying and spoke from heaven through His angel.

"'What is the matter, Hagar? Do not be afraid; God has heard the boy crying as he lies there. Lift the boy up and take him by the hand, for I will make him into a great nation.' Then God opened her eyes and she saw a well of water. So she went and filled the skin with water and gave the boy a drink. God was with the boy as he grew up. He lived in the desert and became an archer. While he was living in the Desert of Paran, his mother got a wife for him from Egypt" (21:17-21). God can create happy endings out of the most painful afflictions!

There's a valuable truth to be absorbed from the statement that "God opened her eyes and she saw a well of water." That well was clearly there all along. But it wasn't clear to Hagar until the Almighty opened her eyes. Many times the Lord's provision for our need is right in front of us, yet we don't recognize it until He opens our eyes. We're inclined to despair much too quickly. The late evangelist Kathryn Kuhlman used to open every one of her daily radio broadcasts with a powerful encouraging reminder. "Remember, just as long as God is still on His throne and hears and answers prayer, and just so long as your faith in Him is still intact, everything will come out all right!"

Beginning at verse 22, Abraham's story introduces us to what can happen to those in whose lives the blessings of God are manifest. Abraham had been somewhat dishonest with Abimelech, yet the king clearly recognized him as a uniquely righteous man who was under the care and protection of the Almighty. Abimelech and Phicol, the commander of his army, paid a visit to Abraham to acknowledge this unusual divine relationship, and seek camaraderie with this friend of God.

"God is with you in everything you do. Now swear to me here before God that you will not deal falsely with me or my children or my descendants. Show to me and the country where you are living as an alien the same kindness I have shown to you" (21:22,23). Those who don't really know the Lord are often drawn to those whose walk with Him demonstrates the benefits of faith in God. Abimelech sought secondary gain from a relationship with one of God's own children. He would have done better to pursue the fuller blessings which flow from a personal relationship with the one true God Himself.

Abraham swore to show kindness to Abimelech and his extended family, then went on to raise the issue of a well that some of the kings' servants had stolen from him. Abimelech responded by saying that this was the first he'd heard of the matter, but soon addressed it properly. Abraham gave livestock to Abimelech (perhaps sacrificing them as the seal of a blood covenant) and the two of them made a treaty.

The patriarch then additionally provided seven ewe lambs to the king, a move which initially puzzled Abimelech. When asked why he did this, Abraham urged his newly established treaty partner to accept the lambs as a witness that the disputed well belonged to himself. Abimelech accepted Abraham's gift and his claim to have dug the well. That location was named "Beersheba" in honor of the agreement. Centuries later it became the southernmost town in Israel. Beersheba can mean either "the well of seven" or "the well of the oath."

Upon conclusion of the interchange, Abimelech and Phicol returned to their headquarters and Abraham celebrated on the spot by planting a tamarisk tree and calling on the name of "Yahweh, the Eternal God." He recognized that it was the benevolent influence of the Lord which had brought about this peaceful relationship with a powerful neighbor. The tamarisk tree was symbolic of the shelter and shade Abraham had found under the care of his God.

The narrative of Abraham's second encounter with Abimelech ends with the statement: "And Abraham stayed in the land of the Philistines for a long time" (21:34). It's useful to note here that the "Philistines" represented by Abimelech and his people are likely a different clan than that of the same name which later populated the area and became avowed enemies of the Israelites. Both Scriptural accounts, and those of extra-biblical historical sources, support this view.

We move on to Genesis chapter 22, which documents what I believe is the story that marks the very pinnacle of Abraham's trek of faith. Hebrews chapter 11 (which we noted in chapter 1 of our book is often referred to as "Faith's Hall of Fame") cites three events in the life of Abraham which illustrate his great trust in God. The first two are his willingness to leave the place where his family had settled in Haran for a strange land the Lord would later show him, and then he and Sarah having a son together in spite of his being past age and her being barren. Here in Genesis 22 is the original account of the final of these three examples of his faith listed in Hebrews 11.

We don't know exactly when this particular episode took place. The account simply begins by informing us that *some time later* God tested Abraham. In my estimation the word "tested" is an understated introduction to the intensely emotional drama that follows.

The opening word from the Lord to His friend was succinct, as was the man's response. "He said to him, 'Abraham!' 'Here I am,' he replied" (22:1). That's where the simplicity ends and the complexities start. Abraham had no idea what was coming. He just knew that when God called, his responsibility was to make himself available.

I'm sure Abraham could not have imagined the divine instructions that immediately ensued. To us who stand at a distance today, they're unthinkable. To the loving father who stood directly in front of the Almighty in that very moment, God's commands must have thrust like a dagger into his heart with such shock and pain that it figuratively, if not literally, brought him to his knees. "Then God said, 'Take your son, your only son, Isaac, whom you love, and go to the region of Moriah. Sacrifice him there as a burnt offering on one of the mountains I will tell you about'" (22:2).

The Bible references no immediate verbal, or even internal emotional, reaction from Abraham. Still, In such circumstances I can't conceive of any human being, no matter how fully surrendered to God, who wouldn't have a flood of anguished emotions and troubling questions surging within. If the Lord were to ask me to die for Him I would find it very difficult, but my hope and expectation is that in His strength I would be able to do it. However, if He asked me to end the life of one of my children, I doubt

I could do it. I can hardly even envision how incredibly painful that very idea would be.

Then there is the question of how a loving God could demand the killing of one's own child as an act of worship? In Scripture the Lord condemns those who sacrificed their children on the altars of cruel false gods. How could He then command His servant to do the same at an altar constructed for worship of Yahweh Himself? Further, Abraham may have wondered how God could possibly fulfill His promise to continue the covenant with his descendants through Isaac if Isaac were *dead*. How?

These are all disturbing quandaries. This divine command seemed to defy not only human logic, but the very just and loving nature of the God who gave that command! Obeying the Word of the Lord often requires our faith to stretch far beyond our understanding.

We have only theorized about Abraham's possible thoughts and words in the moments that followed God's epic directives. Genesis reveals nothing on that matter. What it does tell us is that he quickly acted in obedience... amazing! "Early the next morning Abraham got up and saddled his donkey. He took with him two of his servants and his son Isaac. When he had cut enough wood for the burnt offering, he set out for the place God had told him about" (22:3).

Three days later Abraham looked ahead and recognized in the distance the destination the Lord had ordained for the sacrifice. He told his servants: "...Stay here with the donkey while I and the boy go over there. We will worship and then we will come back to you" (22:5). This statement raises a question, and establishes a remarkable possibility.

How old was Isaac? Here, and in verse 12, he's referred to as a "boy." The use of this English word immediately causes us to imagine that he was of an age at which we would consider him still a child. The word in the original Hebrew text, however, is more ambiguous than that. "Na'ar" can mean "a boy, a youth, or a young adult." So since there is no mention of his age, or the precise timeline of this event in the text, we can only speculate. Many scholars believe he was likely in his twenties. Two things we can plainly determine is that Isaac was physically strong enough to carry a load of wood, and advanced enough in his thinking to understand what a burnt offering was (see verse 7).

The extraordinary truth unveiled in the above quoted text is that Abraham expected to return to his servants with Isaac *alive!* In faith he declared: _we will worship and we will come back to you_. This fact is clarified by the recounting of this event in Hebrews 11:19. "Abraham reasoned that God could raise the dead, and figuratively speaking, he did receive Isaac back from death." Yahweh had not specifically told Abraham that He would resurrect Isaac after the sacrifice, but the man so firmly believed the promise of God that his descendants would come through Isaac, that if the Giver of Life had to raise him from the dead to accomplish that, He would perform the miracle!

Father and son divided between them the load of materials needed for the sacrifice, and headed up the mountainside. Isaac was puzzled about something, and on the way up he sought an answer from his father. "'The fire and wood are here,' Isaac said, 'but where is the lamb for the burnt offering?'" (22:7).

Obviously Abraham had not told Isaac that God had

instructed him to sacrifice his "only son." Had the patriarch shared this fact with anyone else... even Sarah or the servants who accompanied him on this journey? Probably he had not. Sometimes certain communications between the Lord and His individual children should remain private.

The anguished father's response to Isaac's inquiry was evasive but true. "Abraham answered, 'God himself will provide the lamb for the burnt offering, my son.' And the two of them went on together" (22:8). It appears no further weighty conversations took place between the covenant father and the son of promise for the reminder of the climb.

Upon arrival at the location the Lord had designated, the pair set about the sacred preparations. The altar was built and the fuel for the fire placed on it. Then came two of the most heart-rending measures for Abraham. He tied Isaac up and placed him on the altar. It now was clear to the son that he was the lamb for the burnt offering. Though he had to have been fearful of his fate, there's no mention of any resistance on his part. He must have been submissive to his earthly father, and thus submissive to the will of the Heavenly Father as well.

Sound familiar? The parallels between this event and another one two-thousand years later are undeniable. An only Son became a sacrificial lamb. Though He too struggled with the pain of the fate that awaited Him, He also surrendered to His Father's will. Even the mountain where the twin events took place many centuries apart was likely the same. II Chronicles 3:1 identifies Mount Moriah as being located in Jerusalem. And whether figuratively or literally, both deaths were superseded by resurrections!

Isaac now upon the altar, Abraham took the weapon of death in his hand and was about to plunge it into his beloved son, when a welcome intervention occurred. "But the angel of the LORD called out to him from heaven, 'Abraham! Abraham!' 'Here I am,' he replied. 'Do not lay a hand on the boy,' he said. 'Do not do anything to him. Now I know that you fear God, because you have not withheld from me your son, your only son'" (22:11,12).

Knowing that the "angel of the LORD" is commonly considered by many Bible scholars to be an appearance of the Son of God on earth prior to His incarnation centuries later as Jesus of Nazareth, it's amazing to think of the implications of such an appearance. Christ would have been on earth witnessing and responding to an event which foreshadowed His own sacrificial death to redeem mankind!

Abraham had been fully obedient to God's commands. We know that it took great faith to do what he did. But here we learn that it was not only his *faith in God* which proved to be pleasing to the Lord, but his *fear of God* as well. The indispensable fact that reverential fear of God is the foundation of knowledge and wisdom is repeated many places in the Word of God.

Yet while we hear much preaching and teaching on the subject of *faith* (as we should), we hear little about that of *fear.* Reverential fear of the Almighty is essential to our walk with God. Have we put too much emphasis upon the Lord's love, mercy, and grace; and too little upon His holiness, justice, and even His righteous anger? Abraham's consideration of both, enabled him to emerge from his darkest night of testing into his most brilliant morning of rejoicing!

SAM MASON

The Lord was not actually requiring him to sacrifice his son, but was testing him to see if he would be willing to do so in obedience to the command of God. Thus having already inwardly surrendered Isaac to the Lord, Abraham did not have to do so outwardly. He had passed the test.

I'm reminded of a time during my training for ministry when God was testing me. It was not an issue so momentous as that facing Abraham. Still, I could begin to grasp the inward struggle faced by the servant of the Lord. The Holy Spirit had begun tugging at my heart about becoming a foreign missionary.

I did not want to leave my homeland, and was frankly afraid of such a call. The inner conflict went on for months until I finally resolved that if this were my calling, I would obey the Lord despite my fears. I finally surrendered and told God that I was willing to go to the mission field. The moment my heart fully yielded, the Lord spoke to me and said He was not sending me overseas, He just wanted to know that I was willing to go.

Lesson learned, right? Wrong. A little later during my Bible school years, God asked me to give up something I really wanted. The idea of doing so was painful. But I recalled my previous battle of wills with the Lord and decided to surrender once more.

I expected Him to say everything was okay now, and I could have what I wanted so badly. He just needed to know that I was willing to release it to Him. But this time was different. The surrender was to become a full reality. He was actually making me give it up to Him. Sometimes our spiritual tests are inward only. Other times they're meant to produce outward fruit as well.

Back to Abraham's story. Having at the last moment

prevented him from sacrificing Isaac, the Almighty then furnished an animal for the burnt offering. The patriarch collected the ram he'd found with it's horns tangled in a nearby thicket, and sacrificed it upon the altar. In view of all which proceeded it, that act of worship had to be incredibly heartening and gratifying.

Abraham gave that place a special name: Yahweh-Yireh (previously pronounced Jehovah-Jireh), meaning: the Lord will provide. "And to this day it is said, 'On the mountain of the LORD it will be provided'" (22:14). In other words, this expression became a Jewish proverb. It can well be an adage to us today too. It's often in the full surrender of true worship that we discover God's provision for our need.

Shortly after God's arrival on the scene to stop the killing of Isaac and provide a ram instead, He spoke to Abraham once more from heaven. "I swear by myself, declares the LORD, that because you have done this and have not withheld your son, your only son, I will surely bless you and make your descendants as numerous as the stars in the sky and as the sand on the seashore. Your descendants will take possession of the cities of their enemies, and through your offspring all nations on earth will be blessed, because you have obeyed me" (22:16-18).

The obedience which flows from real faith results in rewards for God's children. Those rewards can reach beyond the individual believer to our circle of family and friends, and even the world around us. Yahweh reaffirmed his covenant promises to Abraham, this time sealing them with an oath! The faith of God's friend had ascended to a joyful apex! Father and son re-joined the servants in the valley below, then headed for home.

The final verses of chapter 22 reveal information that paves the way for the last major event in the life of Abraham: the securing of a godly wife for his son of promise. Verse 23 in particular introduces us to that woman who will become a pivotal person in the epoch of the early development of God's chosen people. Her name is Rebekah.

But first the name of another important woman in our story arises again. Genesis chapter 23 opens with the news of the passing of one who might well be called: *the first lady of the faith*. "Sarah lived to be a hundred and twenty-seven years old. She died at Kiriath Arba (that is, Hebron) in the land of Canaan, and Abraham went to mourn for Sarah and to weep over her" (23:1,2). By the way, she is the only woman in all of Scripture whose age is ever mentioned.

While Abraham is widely considered the *father of the faithful*, his beloved wife is in essence described in one New Testament passage as the *mother of faithful women*. In holding Sarah up as a model, and speaking to women about her in I Peter 3:6, it says: "You are her daughters if you do what is right and do not give way to fear."

Like her husband, she was imperfect, but in spite of her battles with doubts and anxieties, she did "not give way to fear," but held on to the promises of God. In doing so she became not only Isaac's mother, but the mother of all Israel. Abraham had a number of other children, but only the one from Sarah's womb would be the ancestor of God's chosen people. Beyond that, the Word of God declares that Abraham's fatherhood reaches to those under the new covenant as well as the old one. Galatians 3:29 says: "If you belong to Christ, then you are Abraham's seed, and heirs according to the promise." That being so, we might very well say that Sarah's motherhood reaches to those under the new covenant too.

The remainder of chapter 23 chronicles Abraham's purchase of a grave for Sarah. Verses 3 and 4 begin by telling us that after grieving for some time, he "...arose from beside his dead wife and spoke to the Hittites. He said, 'I am a stranger among you. Sell me some property for a burial site here so I can bury my dead.'"

The wording seems to imply that his Hittite neighbors had already gathered around him to offer their sympathy. He had lived among them in such a way that they had developed great appreciation and respect for him. In their initial reply to his request they expressed high esteem for Abraham. They referred to him as "a mighty prince among us." The title "mighty prince" literally means "prince of God." They recognized Abraham's righteous life and the resultant rich blessings of the Lord upon him. May the same be true of all believers.

We won't get into the details of the extensive but friendly negotiations which took place between Abraham and his neighbors, except to say that he eventually bought a field from Ephron the Hittite and placed Sarah's body in a cave on that property. We might ask why Abraham had to purchase this field when it was part of the land of Canaan the Lord had promised to him. We need to understand that the divine deeding of the Promised Land was primarily to his descendants. He clearly understood this. In speaking to his chief servant about it later, Abraham quoted Yahweh directly on the issue. "To your *offspring* I will give this land" (Genesis 24:7). That actual possession was not achieved until after the Israelites returned to Canaan from Egypt centuries later.

The cave at Machpelah eventually became the burial site of not only Sarah, but also Abraham, Isaac, Jacob, and their wives. The only exception was Jacob's wife, Rachael, who had been buried near Bethlehem. To this day the cave at Machpelah is an honored and frequently visited memorial in the heart of the Israeli city of Hebron.

The Bible account of Abraham's plans to get a wife for Isaac is preceded briefly by a statement proclaiming how God had given him a long life filled with divine benefits. "Abraham was now old and well advanced in years, and the LORD had blessed him in every way" (Genesis 24:1). These are the benefits afforded to a man who continued to pursue the Lord throughout his lifetime, never allowing the enemy to use his trying circumstances or personal failures to persuade him to abandon that pursuit. His faithful quest bore much fruit; blessings in every way!

Because he wanted the blessings of heaven to rain upon his son also, he determined to find him a spouse who would be a help, rather than a hindrance in his spiritual journey. Probably because of the physical limitations of his age Abraham summoned his trusted head servant to assign the task to him. This steward of the household may have been Eliezer of Damascus, mentioned in Genesis 15:2. Clearly the man was someone in whom Abraham had great confidence. He had made him "the one in charge of all that he had" (24:2). As this story unfolds, we'll see that his confidence was well placed.

The gravity of this assignment was such that Abraham began the conversation by insisting upon an oath of solemn commitment. "I want you to swear by the LORD, the God of heaven and the God of earth, that you will not get a wife for my son from the daughters of the Canaanites, among whom I am living, but will go to my country and my own relatives and get a wife for my son Isaac" (24:3,4).

I'm convinced that the patriarch's preeminent concern that Isaac's wife come from his relatives rather than the neighboring Canaanites, is based upon the desire for spiritual compatibility, not familial bonds or ethnic purity. While there is no explicit notation of it in Scripture, there is evidence that Abraham's relatives back in Mesopotamia may also have been worshipers of Yahweh. On the other hand, the Canaanites were obviously pagans. If his son were to follow in the ways of the Lord, he needed a companion who also believed in the only true God and would serve Him wholeheartedly.

Abraham's servant was willing to agree to this stipulation, but had a question about a possible contingency. "The servant asked him, 'What if the woman is unwilling to come back with me to this land? Shall I then take your son back to the country you came from?'" (24:5). This servant had the wisdom to look ahead and foresee potential problems, and the faithfulness to his master to ask what his will might be in such a situation. The response was quick and certain. "'Make sure that you do not take my son back there,' Abraham said" (24:6). As referenced earlier, the aged father quoted God's promise to give the land of Canaan to his offspring. Faith in, and obedience to, the Word of the Lord was paramount.

Abraham's next words remind me of the confession of the three Hebrew children when faced with a horrible death in Nebuchadnezzar's fiery furnace for refusing to bow down before an idol. They told the king that they were confident that God could save them from certain death, but even if He didn't, they would never disobey the Lord!

The friend of God declared his trust in the Lord of Heaven to his chief servant. "...He will send his angel before you so that you can get a wife for my son from there. If the woman is unwilling to come back with you, then you will be released from this oath of mine. Only do not take my son back there" (24:7,8). Like Shadrach, Meshach, Abednego, and Abraham, there are times when we must act in line with God's will even when we don't know for certain exactly what the outcome will be.

The servant agreed to fully comply with all that was stipulated, and according to the custom of the day, placed his hand under his master's thigh and swore an oath to carry out his orders. He wasted no time in getting underway, gathering ten camels, travel provisions, valuable gifts for the bride-to-be, and other household servants needed as manpower for the trip. He quickly set out for Aram Naharaim, the area of northwest Mesopotamia where most of Abraham's family had settled years earlier near Haran.

No details of the of the journey itself are provided. They eventually arrived in the hometown of Nahor, Abraham's brother, near dusk one evening, just at the time women were heading out to draw water from the local well. There the chief servant had the camels kneel down, and there he prayed a prayer for clear direction from God.

Abraham's faithful servant did what we for many years have referred to as "laying out a fleece" before the Lord. That phrase describes an act performed by Gideon, a leader of Israel during the period of the judges. You can read the account in Judges chapters 6 and 7. What both men did was to ask God for specific signs which would assure them that He was speaking to them in a manner that left no question that the Almighty was at work.

"Then he prayed, 'O LORD, God of my master Abraham, give me success today, and show kindness to my master Abraham. See, I am standing beside this spring, and the daughters of the townspeople are coming out to draw water. May it be that when I say to a girl, 'Please let down your jar that I may have a drink,' and she says, 'Drink, and I'll water your camels too'—let her be the one you have chosen for your servant Isaac. By this I will know that you have shown kindness to my master'" (24:12-14).

There are times when we must wait patiently for answers to prayer. This was not one of those times. "Before he had finished praying, Rebekah came out with her jar on her shoulder. She was the daughter of Bethuel son of Milcah, who was the wife of Abraham's brother Nahor. The girl was very beautiful, a virgin; no man had ever lain with her. She went down to the spring, filled her jar and came up again" (24:15,16).

Abraham's servant rushed to her side and asked her for a drink of water. From that moment on, everything went just as he had prayed it would. On her own initiative the lovely young maiden drew enough water for all ten of the camels… an amount which could easily have totaled more than a hundred gallons! This girl was not only beautiful and chaste, but remarkably humble, kind, and hard-working as well. The visitor from the land of Canaan observed her quietly and carefully, as Rebekah fulfilled before his very eyes all the confirming signs that he'd requested of God.

He had to have been feeling a mounting sense of

anticipation. It certainly looked like the Lord was truly guiding him. In appreciation for the young woman's commendable efforts he gave her a generous gift of gold jewelry. Then came the questions which could provide the final confirmation that this was the wife God had chosen for Isaac. "Whose daughter are you? Please tell me, is there room in your father's house for us to spend the night?" (24:23).

Her response brought great joy to his heart! "She answered him, 'I am the daughter of Bethuel, the son that Milcah bore to Nahor.' And she added, 'We have plenty of straw and fodder, as well as room for you to spend the night'" (24:24,25). Abraham's servant immediately bowed in worship of Yahweh. "Praise be to the LORD, the God of my master Abraham, who has not abandoned his kindness and faithfulness to my master. As for me, the LORD has led me on the journey to the house of my master's relatives" (24:27).

His excitement became *her* excitement. Rebekah ran home and shared the news with those of her mother's household. When her brother, Laban, heard what had happened and saw the jewelry on his sister, he ran to the well to welcome this stranger who was servant to his grandfather's brother.

Happily accepting the invitation, Abraham's servant arrived and received the promised hospitality. The camels were unloaded and fed, and according to the custom of the day, he and his attendants were given water to wash their feet. A meal was set before them. Although they were likely quite hungry from the journey, the servant felt strongly that something else was more pressing than his hunger. He must first tell them why he was there.

His responsibility to his master took precedence over everything else. Sensing his urgency, Laban gave him permission to speak what was on his heart.

He recounted the entire story, beginning with the abundant blessings God had bestowed upon his master, making him wealthy, and giving him and Sarah a son in their old age. He related his master's command for him to go back to his homeland to find a wife for that son of promise, and how he had made him swear an oath to do everything just as Abraham had instructed him. He included the vital detail that the bride and her family must grant permission for the marriage. Otherwise, he would be released from his oath.

The faithful servant went on to tell of what had happened at the well earlier that day. He had asked the Lord for specific signs so he would know of a certainty that he'd found the right woman. God had confirmed that Rebekah was the one, and now he needed to know if she and her family would consent to her move to Canaan and marriage to Isaac. Where events would go from here was dependent upon their decision. Nothing mattered more than this. God's will may be plainly revealed, but we are still free moral agents and must choose to submit to it.

In this case, not only was Rebekah willing to do God's bidding, those in authority over her in that culture, her father and brother, wholeheartedly agreed. Their verbal response offered no resistance whatsoever to the divine plan. "Laban and Bethuel answered, 'This is from the LORD; we can say nothing to you one way or the other. Here is Rebekah; take her and go, and let her become the wife of your master's son, as the LORD has directed'" (24:50,51).

Abraham's servant once again fell down and worshiped Yahweh for His goodness. Then he gave costly gifts to Rebekah: more jewelry, and additionally some rich clothing. The ring and bracelets previously given were a reward for her acts of kindness. These presents were bridal in nature. His task had been successful because God had answered his and his master's prayers. Finally he and his men were ready to enjoy the meal prepared for them. After what had to have become a celebratory feast, they retired for the night.

Come sunrise a potential hiccup arose. The bride's brother and mother wanted to delay her departure for a while. Having received the Lord's stamp of approval and the consent of her and her family for the marriage to Isaac, the chief servant asked that they send him and the bride on their way that morning as they'd planned. Rebekah's brother and mother called her and placed the issue in her lap. Her decision was prompt and her words simple. "I will go" (24:57).

The family sent Rebekah, her nurse, and her maids on their way with a blessing for the bride. "Our sister, may you increase to thousands upon thousands; may your offspring possess the gates of their enemies" (24:60). The latter portion of this blessing was nearly word for word that given by the Lord to Abraham's descendants in Genesis 22:17.

The caravan arrived in the Negev area of the Promised Land where Isaac had moved from Beer La-hai Roi. At that moment, he had been out in the field meditating. It was a moment of destiny. "...As he looked up, he saw camels approaching. Rebekah also looked up and saw Isaac. She got down from her camel and asked the servant,

'Who is that man in the field coming to meet us?' 'He is my master,' the servant answered. So she took her veil and covered herself" (24:63-65). In this moment the bride was properly attired for her groom.

Abraham's servant was now Isaac's servant as well. He caught Isaac up to date on all that had transpired during his absence, especially how God had unmistakably borne witness to the fact that Rebekah was His choice for Isaac. Apparently no time was wasted. "Isaac brought her into the tent of his mother Sarah, and he married Rebekah. So she became his wife, and he loved her; and Isaac was comforted after his mother's death" (24:67).

We're not told Rebekah's age, but Genesis 25:20 indicates Isaac was forty when they married. This would have been roughly three years after Sarah's death, which is why Isaac's grief was soothed by his marriage to Rebekah. Sarah's dwelling had likely been empty since her passing. By escorting her into his mother's tent, Isaac was declaring that Rebekah was now matriarch of the clan. At his earthly father's command, the chief servant had been led by the Heavenly Father to provide a lovely god-fearing woman to continue the covenant line of God's chosen people.

The first 11 verses of Genesis chapter 25 conclude the saga of God's friend, Abraham. It starts with the mention of his final wife (or concubine), Keturah, and their children. Although there's no time frame established, it's generally considered that Abraham married Keturah at some point following Sarah's passing. Their six sons and the ethnology of a few of their further generations are listed. As with Ishmael's descendants, they may be connected with the Arab people.

It's noted that while Abraham gave gifts to the sons of his concubines, the bulk of his possessions were passed on to Isaac. As the son of promise, he was the heir to all of Abraham's remaining estate. Like Ishmael before them, the others were eventually sent away to the east. According to God's plan, the promised land of Canaan was reserved only for Isaac and his progeny.

The details surrounding the death of Abraham are recorded in verses 7 though 11. He lived to be 175 years old. Verse 8 describes his passing as follows: "Then Abraham breathed his last and died at a good old age, an old man and full of years; and he was gathered to his people." Two salient facts are communicated in this verse. The first pertains to his lifespan. God had blessed him with a long life. The phrases "good old age" and "full of years" indicate the kind of earthly existence the Lord intends for the righteous. Although there are obviously exceptions to this principle, it is a general rule. In Psalm 91:16 God says of the person who loves Him: "With long life will I satisfy him and show him my salvation."

The second fact pertains to life after our earthly sojourn: "He was gathered to his people." This Scriptural phrase and others similar to it throughout the Old Testament, point not only to a common earthly burial, but even more so to the expectation of an afterlife reunion with family who've gone on before. Best of all, it anticipates the entrance to an eternity in the Presence of our Heavenly Father! This is the heritage of all who trust in the Lord.

Verse 9 chronicles the coupling of Isaac and Ishmael to mourn the death and honor the life of their mutual father, Abraham. We're not told how broad the scope of this get-together of half-brothers may have been, but at the very least they shared a love and respect for their father. Even if Ishmael did not enjoy the level of familial distinction that belonged to Isaac, and did not share in the Abrahamic Covenant, he was the son of Abraham and was under a divine blessing of his own. Thus he and his half-brother were the only ones among the patriarch's offspring noted as overseeing their father's burial. The final resting place of the patriarch's body was in the cave at Machpelah where Sarah had been interred some 38 years earlier.

The concluding statement in the story of Abraham's demise relates the passing of the covenant torch. "After Abraham's death, God blessed his son Isaac, who then lived near Beer Lahai Roi" (25:11). All of us want to leave a legacy, particularly to our family. May that legacy be the example of the blessing of God which attends the living of a righteous life of faith.

In looking back and evaluating the life of Abraham, we observe what we've noted in the title of this chapter: he was *imperfect, but faithful.* When he veered off course, he climbed back onto the highway to heaven. Yes, he was *in* this world... but never *of* this world. "By faith he made his home in the promised land like a stranger in a foreign country; he lived in tents, as did Isaac and Jacob, who were heirs with him of the same promise. For he was looking forward to the city with foundations, whose architect and builder is God" (Hebrews 11:9,10).

Despite his imperfections, he remained a stranger to this rebellious world, and the friend of God. Abraham's over-riding purpose in life was not to absorb the pleasures and values of the prevailing culture, but to honor God through faith and obedience. James 4:4 declares that we cannot be a true friend of God and attach ourselves to a godless society at the same time. "Anyone who chooses to be a friend of the world becomes an enemy of God." In various places throughout the Gospel of John, Jesus declared that He, His Kingdom, and His disciples were *not of this world.*

As we consider Abraham's righteous life, two undeniable Scriptural truths that relate to us as well as him, confront us. Number one, we're *perfect* in our *standing* before God from the very moment we put our faith in Him. The blood of Christ purifies us from all sin (see I John 1:7). This is salvation. Number two, we're *imperfect* in our *state* even while we pursue functional perfection. We should be becoming more like Jesus with the passing of the years (see II Corinthians 3:18 and Philippians 3:12-14). This is sanctification. Salvation is a once in a lifetime transaction. Sanctification is a lifelong process.

Abraham's spiritual journey illustrates these divine principles. He put his faith in the Lord and set out to follow Him. Along the way he stumbled and failed. Like all of us who become believers, he sinned at times. But God was always merciful and Abraham always got up and moved onward and upward. Through all of his shortcomings he never turned his heart away from God. Over the years he continued to grow in grace. Though imperfect, he was faithful to the call. That's why Abraham is considered "the father of the faithful."

Chapter 4

Lot: Imperfect and Prone to Wander

In chapter 1 of this book we established that Lot was Abraham's nephew, that he was a righteous man, and that by faith he chose to join Abraham's pilgrimage to the land the Lord had promised to show him. The younger half of the duo of righteous men featured in this story had made a wise and godly decision to follow not only the path of his pious uncle, but what was truly the leading of the Lord Himself.

It's very possible that when he left Haran to obey Yahweh's command, Abraham had invited numerous other family members to accompany him. Lot, however, was the only one to bond with him in his pursuit of the blessed life of a loving relationship with the Almighty. Lot had already chosen Abraham as his father figure in the *social sense*. In choosing to become his companion in following God, he'd made Abraham his *spiritual* father too.

Unfortunately as we'll discover, Lot would gradually

diverge from that road of rich blessing. That divergence would seem to have begun sometime after he and Abraham returned from their stay in Egypt. Both of them had prospered greatly over time. This is an illustration of the truth of Proverbs 10:22, which declares: "The blessing of the LORD brings wealth, and adds no trouble to it."

But fallen humanity often forges its own trouble even in the midst of blessing, and their wealth eventually led to conflict. "Now Lot, who was moving about with Abram, also had flocks and herds and tents. But the land could not support them while they stayed together, for their possessions were so great that they were not able to stay together. And quarreling arose between Abram's herdsmen and the herdsmen of Lot. The Canaanites and Perizzites were also living in the land at that time" (Genesis 13:5-7).

The angry disputes at that time did not involve Abraham and Lot directly, and did not appear to have risen to the level of violence, but there was concern that they could spread and escalate. Then there was the complicating factor of the local inhabitants: the Canaanites and Perizzites. Why were they mentioned? I can conceive of at least three reasons. First, their presence in the area could have provided even more claims on the land, potentially adding to the territorial contentions. Secondly, these pagan groups might eventually get involved in any armed conflict which broke out. And thirdly, It would be a bad witness to outsiders for believing brethren to fight among themselves.

In view of these troubling possibilities, Abraham initiated a summit with his nephew. The patriarch's approach to the issue was notably altruistic. "So Abram said to Lot, 'Let's not have any quarreling between you and me, or between your herdsmen and mine, for we are brothers. Is not the whole land before you? Let's part company. If you go to the left, I'll go to the right; if you go to the right, I'll go to the left'" (13:8,9). The choice was rightly Abraham's. Not only should he have been the honored elder of the pair, he was the one to whose descendants God had promised this whole land. The divine right to Canaan had been sovereignly bestowed upon his offspring (see Genesis 12:7).

On the other hand, Lot's reaction to his uncle's generous proposal was selfish and materialistic. He expressed no reluctance over the suggestion that he and his godly mentor part company. His response reflected more interest in earthly things than spiritual concerns. Here we catch our initial glimpse of Lot's dangerous worldly tendencies.

"Lot looked up and saw that the whole plain of the Jordan was well watered, like the garden of the LORD, like the land of Egypt, toward Zoar. (This was before the LORD destroyed Sodom and Gomorrah.) So Lot chose for himself the whole plain of the Jordan and set out toward the east" (13:10,11). The comparison of the Jordan valley to not only the Garden of Eden, but the land of Egypt, probably stemmed from Lot's experience there when Abraham and he escaped the famine in Canaan at the time and found plenty in Egypt. Again, we get the feeling that his priority seemed to be physical sustenance rather than spiritual growth.

As we noted before, both men had already been blessed materially. Yet there is a clear distinction in their attitudes toward these *things*. There's no record that Abraham ever pursued such blessings. He simply walked with God in faith and obedience, and the material blessings flowed from the hand of the Lord. Lot though, became enamored with these *things* by succumbing to the lust of the eyes. He "looked up and saw" a very fertile portion of the land that appeared to offer great abundance and stunning external beauty. Abraham sought God and received prosperity. Lot sought opulence and began to wander away from God's best.

It's important here to take a moment to stress that material prosperity is not a universal or automatic benefit of righteous living. God has promised to bless us and meet our needs, but He has not pledged great earthly wealth to *all* who follow Him. Temporal material blessing is more emphasized under the old covenant, while under the new covenant the emphasis is on eternal spiritual blessings.

The New Testament deals with the issue of monetary riches in a balanced way. Money can be either a blessing or curse. It depends upon what you do with money and what money does with you. Perhaps the bottom line is best represented by what Hebrews 13:5 says. "Keep your lives free from the love of money and be content with what you have, because God has said, 'Never will I leave you; never will I forsake you.'" Temporal wealth is a superficial blessing. Eternal wealth is the abiding Presence of the Lord.

The separation of uncle and nephew is eventually described in Scripture as follows: "The two men parted company: Abram lived in the land of Canaan, while Lot lived among the cities of the plain and pitched his tents near Sodom. Now the men of Sodom were wicked and were sinning greatly against the LORD" (13:11-13).

Abraham's location is described in broad terms as "the land of Canaan" because of his obedience to God's command (in verse 17) that he should continue to move about *through the entire land.* The text indicates that Lot's initial chosen destination was quickly transitioning in a disturbing way. He'd originally decided upon the "whole *plain of the Jordan* and set out toward the *east.*" But he ended up moving more south than east, settling "among the cities of the plain," and pitching "his tents near Sodom." Lot was moving not only toward potentially greater material prosperity, but toward a more wicked environment.

This is a path of spiritual regression aptly described in Psalm 1:1. There we're advised to avoid this pattern if we want to live in the blessings of the Lord. "Blessed is the man who does not walk in the counsel of the wicked or stand in the way of sinners or sit in the seat of mockers."

I've often characterized this verse as describing "three steps to a cynic." The decline begins with allowing the philosophy of a wicked culture to negatively influence our biblical belief system. Then we start to live among unbelievers, slowly adopting their lifestyle. Finally, if we continue in this destructive path, we totally reject divine truth and turn our backs on God. This relapse is further illustrated by the successive use of the words: *walk, stand, sit.* Our spiritual movement diminishes until it finally comes to a total halt! Psalm 1 goes on to contrast these cancerous consequences with the healthy benefits of walking in the ways of the Lord.

While we witness the moral decline of Lot and his family over the course of this story, we need to continually remind ourselves that he is *not a pagan*. This is a righteous man, a saint who has put his faith in the living God. Every time believers make a decision to compromise with the worldly system, we risk ultimately losing our own righteous identity … and even that of our families… to the alluring deception of sin.

As Lot moved away toward the personally appealing land he had observed with his earthly vision, God instructed Abraham to view something too. "The LORD said to Abram after Lot had parted from him, 'Lift up your eyes from where you are and look north and south, east and west. All the land that you see I will give to you and your offspring forever. I will make your offspring like the dust of the earth, so that if anyone could count the dust, then your offspring could be counted. Go, walk through the length and breadth of the land, for I am giving it to you'" (13:14-17).

So in obedience, Abraham commenced his lifelong exploration of the promised land. He never built a permanent home. He was a pilgrim not only in Canaan, but upon the earth itself. "So Abram moved his tents and went to live near the great trees of Mamre at Hebron, where he built an altar to the LORD" (13:18). The only enduring structures he left behind wherever he stayed were those he used to worship his God. Sadly, there's no record of Lot doing the same in his new location.

Genesis chapter 14 introduces us to the first outwardly negative result of Lot's relocation. We should preface the report of this incident by noting that he had by now moved from *near* Sodom to *within* the wicked city itself (see 14:12). He was step by step continuing to stray further away from divine truth, and closer to the error and deception of the enemy.

We won't take up space here to list all the details of the various kingly alliances involved in a war which eventually left Lot and his family temporary captives. Suffice it to say that four kings had previously invaded the domain of five others (including Sodom and Gomorrah) and had kept them under subjugation for a dozen years. Then the five attempted to throw off the control of the four. Responding to that rebellion, these four rulers eventually went on a rampage, conquering other kingdoms throughout the region. Following that, the five kings (including those of Sodom and Gomorrah) who had already been under the control of the four, went to war against those four others, drawing up battle lines in the Valley of Siddim (meaning "valley of salt," signifying the area surrounding the Dead Sea).

The ensuing conflict did not go well for the alliance led by Sodom and Gomorrah. Their troops ran from the fight. Some of them fell into the tar pits which littered the valley. Those who didn't get trapped in such sticky craters fled to the hills. That left the inhabitants remaining in the two wicked cities virtually unprotected. "The four kings seized all the goods of Sodom and Gomorrah and all their food; then they went away. They also carried off Abram's nephew Lot and his possessions, since he was living in Sodom" (14:11,12).

The capture of Lot in the confines of Sodom itself raises a question. Why was he not out with the soldiers of Sodom, joined in battle against their enemies? The possible answers are numerous. Lot may not have been considered a citizen of that city. Perhaps he was too old to join the fight, or was untrained in military skills. Maybe he refused to defend that town because of its wildly sinful nature. It could be that he stayed behind to better protect his wife and daughters. Or was he simply acting like a coward?

The context provides no definitive explanation. I confess that I don't with any certainty know why he remained within the city limits during the combat. I suspect, however, that the most likely reason is that he was not considered a citizen of that society. Later, in Genesis 19:9, the men of Sodom angrily proclaimed that Lot was an "alien." That same injustice is foisted upon Christians in many places around the globe today. Even in America believers are being increasingly stripped of their legal rights because their values are at variance with those of a prevailing culture which seems to be expanding its embrace of wicked dogmas.

An escapee brought word of the plundering of Sodom and Gomorrah to Abraham, who at the time was living near the great trees of Mamre. The patriarch had developed a friendship with Mamre and his brothers, Eschol and Aner, a bond which would prove particularly valuable in this instance. Upon hearing of Lot's capture, Abraham immediately set out to rescue him.

A rather amazing fact is revealed in verse 14. "...He called out the 318 trained men born in his household and went in pursuit as far as Dan." In human terms the size of Abraham's estate was obviously massive. With 318 battle ready men in his camp, we can determine that his household easily encompassed in excess of a thousand people... probably much more. God had truly blessed and prospered Abraham!

Allied with the aforementioned three Amorite brothers, Lot's uncle entered the fray determined to save Lot and his family. This was no leisurely hike. Abraham and his troops traveled more than a hundred miles in pursuit of the army of the four kings. Whether obtained from personal experience, the advice of others, or divinely imparted wisdom, Abraham demonstrated military leadership skills as he divided his men into multiple attack groups, commencing the assault under the cover of darkness. The Lord granted him total success. He recovered not only Lot and his possessions, but all the captives and spoils from the initial victory of the four kings over the five.

In the aftermath of his conquest, Abraham was greeted by two kings in the Valley of Shaveh, also known as the King's Valley. This royal duo were the *unnamed* king of Sodom, and Melchizedek, king of Salem. The account of this event discloses the godly values which guided God's friend, and the recognition and blessings which sprung from the living out of those values.

The appearance of the king of Sodom is no surprise. He owed a debt of gratitude to Abraham, plus he needed to accompany his rescued people back to his sovereign realm. But the arrival of Melchizedek on the scene is initially something of a puzzle. He was not ruler of one of the five allies originally on the losing end of the war. The first clue as to why he was there in the Valley of Shaveh is the probable location of that particular valley. The Jewish historian Josephus identifies the King's Valley as roughly a quarter of a mile from Jerusalem. Since Salem was the ancient name of Jerusalem, that means that at that moment Abraham was in Melchizedek's neighborhood.

Melchizedek, who besides being king of Salem was

also "priest of God Most High" (14:18), clearly recognized Abraham as a servant of the Lord. That may have been revealed to him in a prophetic word from Yahweh. He came to the nearby valley to honor Abraham and offer praise to God. "...And he blessed Abram, saying, 'Blessed be Abram by God Most High, Creator of heaven and earth. And blessed be God Most High, who delivered your enemies into your hand'" (14:19,20). Abraham subsequently gave Melchizedek a tithe (tenth) of the spoils of the battle.

The definitive identification of exactly who Melchizedek is, remains a matter of some discussion both in Scripture and among Bible scholars. He plays a pivotal role in this event following Abraham's military victory, so let's look a little more closely into the information about him provided in God's Word.

We begin with his name. It essentially means "righteous king." It can be understood as "king of righteousness," or "my king (that is, the Lord) is righteous" Whatever the precise wording, the implications of this name can be pursued by examining the Bible references to Melchizedek.

There are three Bible books that speak of Melchizedek. The first is the one we're dealing with now here in *Genesis* chapter 14. *Psalm* 110 also briefly mentions him. Finally, Melchizedek is the subject of discussion at various points in chapters 5-7 of the epistle to the *Hebrews*.

In the Genesis record we've already discovered that he was king of Salem (Jerusalem) and priest of God Most High. Jerusalem is central to Old Testament worship and New Testament fulfillment. It was the earthly capitol of the Kingdom of God during most of the history of the nation of Israel, and the special earthly dwelling place of

Yahweh. It was the site of Christ's redemptive death and empowering resurrection, plus the original outpouring of the Holy Spirit at the birth of the church. Melchizedek is the first ruler of Jerusalem ever mentioned in Scripture. Thus he's inextricably tied to the sovereignty and worship of the Creator, and the redemptive work of His Son.

As king of Salem, literally "king of peace," his title evokes a connection with the final name of the coming messiah (Jesus, the Christ) prophetically given in Isaiah 9:6. "For to us a child is born, to us a son is given, and the government will be on his shoulders. And he will be called Wonderful Counselor, Mighty God, Everlasting Father, *Prince of Peace.*" Both as king and priest, Melchizedek is linked to the messiah in Psalm 110:4, and in Hebrews 5:6,10; 6:20; and 7:11-17. His provision of bread and wine and other actions in the Genesis story might also cause him to be seen as a type of Christ.

Some see Melchizedek as simply an historical person who was a righteous ruler and early worshiper of the one true God. Many ancient Jewish rabbis identified him as Seth, the godly son of Noah. Other Christian theologians consider him a *theophany*, a term which refers to a visible or human manifestation of God or His Son. This type of manifestation takes place in a number of instances chronicled in the Old Testament, particularly in those describing such entities as "the angel of the Lord," literally "the angel of Yahweh." Thus a theophany is widely taken to be an appearance of the Son of God on earth before His incarnation as Jesus of Nazareth. Whoever he literally is, Melchizedek is unquestionably at least figuratively connected with Jesus.

Abraham treated this king of Salem, with honor. He

did not do the same with the king of Sodom. His nephew Lot had chosen to live under the influence of a profane culture, subordinate to the jurisdiction of their immoral leader. On the other hand, except for his concerns over Lot and his family who lived there, and his compassionate intercessory prayer for its citizens when it faced imminent judgment from God, Abraham wanted no personal fraternization with that wicked city.

His determination to disassociate himself from a corrupt society is evidenced by his response when Sodom's monarch offered him the opportunity to enrich himself by only returning the citizens he had rescued, while keeping the goods he'd recovered. Here's what Abraham said: "I have raised my hand to the LORD, God Most High, Creator of heaven and earth, and have taken an oath that I will accept nothing belonging to you, not even a thread or the thong of a sandal, so that you will never be able to say, 'I made Abram rich.' I will accept nothing but what my men have eaten and the share that belongs to the men who went with me—to Aner, Eshcol and Mamre. Let them have their share" (14:22-24).

We might have expected that Lot would had learned a critical lesson from that perilous experience he suffered as an inhabitant of Sodom. We could have hoped he'd now be more inclined to follow his uncle's wise example. Lamentably, he continued to remain in that vile environment. That in spite of the fact that II Peter 2:7,8 advises us that he "...was distressed by the filthy lives of lawless men (for that righteous man, living among them day after day, was tormented in his righteous soul by the lawless deeds he saw and heard)." Perhaps he felt he might be able to influence that society for good. Or had he simply become willing to live with their spiritual wickedness in order to share in their material prosperity?

The account in Genesis chapter 19 of Lot's final hours in that wicked city demonstrates that either by their total surrender to sin those people had passed the point of no return, or Lot's righteous witness was not very convincing... or both! The two angels who had accompanied the Lord Himself on His visit with Abraham just prior to the divine judgment against Sodom and Gomorrah, were about to arrive at the city's entrance.

Lot was sitting at the gateway when the pair made their entrance. No one was aware that they were heavenly entities. This is not an entirely unique situation. Note that in the account of the events leading up to the final demise of Sodom and Gomorrah, these two were alternately referred to as "men" and "angels." According to Scripture angels often appear on earth as human beings. Lot was about to become an example of what the writer of Hebrews referred to in chapter 13, verse 2. "Do not forget to entertain strangers, for by so doing some people have entertained angels without knowing it."

In that era the town square was usually situated immediately just inside the city gate. It was a place where various activities took place, including the sale of goods, meetings of the city elders, and informal group conversations. Inns for lodging were not commonly available, and the square was an area where travelers could lodge in the open overnight, or receive a kind invitation from the local citizenry to spend the night in their homes. We're not told why Lot was sitting there that evening, but it may have been for just that latter purpose.

"When he saw them, he got up to meet them and

bowed down with his face to the ground. 'My lords,' he said, 'please turn aside to your servant's house. You can wash your feet and spend the night and then go on your way early in the morning'" (19:1,2). It appears no one else had offered any hospitality to these men. This lack of compassion would be consistent with the previously cited description of Sodom found in Ezekiel 16:49. "She and her daughters were arrogant, overfed and unconcerned; they did not help the poor and needy."

Initially the angels declined Lot's invitation, saying they'd sleep there in the square. Yet Lot persisted passionately, and they eventually accepted his offer. He provided not only an opportunity for some personal hygiene and comfortable sleep, but prepared a meal for them as well. It was not as sumptuous a feast as that they had enjoyed earlier with Abraham, but it did enable them to satisfy any hunger they might have had.

While Lot determined only to courteously host these visitors in his home, the male citizens of the city instead had perverse salacious intentions. "Before they had gone to bed, all the men from every part of the city of Sodom— both young and old—surrounded the house. They called to Lot, 'Where are the men who came to you tonight? Bring them out to us so that we can have sex with them'" (19:4,5). Their wicked desires reached far beyond the pale. Homosexual behavior is in and of itself a sin against God and our bodies that He designed for righteous purposes. These men, however, planned to carry out this wicked conduct upon the visitors against their will. This would have been not just a degenerate sexual sin, but felonious assault as well!

In this episode we catch a glimpse of Lot's internal

spiritual conflicts. He evidences both righteous constraint *and* unholy compromise. Unlike the citizens of Sodom, he was willing to kindly offer food and lodging to the two strangers. When the entire male population of the city demanded he release those visitors into their hands, he stood up against them. "Lot went outside to meet them and shut the door behind him and said, 'No, my friends. Don't do this wicked thing'" (19:7).

Yet while Lot attempted to fend off their planned abuse of his guests, he offered to instead sacrifice his own daughters to their savage sexual lusts. The fact that those young ladies were virgins even though they were engaged to be married, would indicate that Lot and his family were living to a higher moral standard than their neighbors. Still, he was willing to surrender his innocent offspring to such horrific treatment. As such, He was certainly compromising with the popular culture.

As a father of two daughters myself, I can't imagine ever turning them over to a violent mob! No wonder II Peter 2:7 describes Lot as "a righteous man, who was distressed." His carnal and unwise choices had created a conflicted mind, and had begun to point him in wrong directions. His compromises had brought him to the place where he was willing to acquiesce to the acceptability of some level of unrighteousness.

In II Peter 3:17,18 we're warned of the same potential spiritual decline creeping into our own lives. "...Be on your guard so that you may not be carried away by the error of lawless men and fall from your secure position. But grow in the grace and knowledge of our Lord and Savior Jesus Christ."

Like Lot, we must be willing to speak out against sin.

Unlike Lot, we must not be willing to tolerate some sins, while standing against others. That's not to suggest that we expect perfection from fallen human beings. While redeemed by the blood of the Lamb, even Christians are still imperfect. But we must never excuse or ignore certain sins because the secular culture proclaims that they are sanctioned. The old Bible-based attitude is still in effect: "*Hate* sin, *love* the sinner." These emotions are not mutually exclusive. They coexist in the nature of the Creator Himself.

Scholars contend that the code of hospitality in that period of history dictated that Lot protect his guests even at the cost of his daughters' virginity... and perhaps even *their very lives*. But godly and family values must rise above worldly mores. Lot condemned the plans of the Sodomites to physically and sexually violate the guests in his home, but sadly, he was willing accept their doing the same to his daughters.

Lot addressed the angry men outside his home as his "friends." Friendship with unbelievers, however, should never allow us to even tacitly give consent to any of their sins. And as Abraham's nephew was about to discover, when the righteous take a stand against wickedness, such friendship is often vehemently rejected.

"'Get out of our way,' they replied. And they said, 'This fellow came here as an alien, and now he wants to play the judge! We'll treat you worse than them.' They kept bringing pressure on Lot and moved forward to break down the door" (19:9). In warning the men of Sodom against wickedness, Lot was being a true friend. Not all sinners, however, will respond to such exhortation with repentance. Yahweh may have viewed Lot's warning as a crucial admonition that could save these men from the destruction looming on the horizon. The men of Sodom censured that same godly guidance as harsh judgmentalism. Some today would condemn Lot and his kind as "haters."

Jesus was and is the friend of sinners. He forgave sin, but He never ignored it.... He never excused it... He never compromised with it. He didn't hesitate to publicly and privately decry it wherever He found it. Nor should we hold back. Sin is to be testified against. It alienates people from a holy God and dooms them to eternal hell. Sin also hurts innocents around it. As followers of Christ we're obligated to proclaim the facts of life and death as revealed in Scripture. We're urged in Ephesians 4:15 to *speak the truth in love*. As the Lord Jesus Himself taught, it is only through knowing the truth that people can be set free from the bondage of sin (see John 8:32). This is not to suggest that we're meant to constantly hound people over every sin. It's that we be willing to take a stand for righteousness whenever the issue arises.

Lot's plea against the wicked intentions of the men of Sodom went unheeded as they proceeded to attempt to break into his home in order to violate his two house guests. Unbeknownst to Lot at that point, that pair were not just men, but powerful angelic beings. "But the men inside reached out and pulled Lot back into the house and shut the door. Then they struck the men who were at the door of the house, young and old, with blindness so that they could not find the door" (19:10,11). The intended victims were becoming the rescuers.

The next two verses demonstrate the deep and wide potential beneficial effect of righteous people upon their families. "The two men said to Lot, "Do you have anyone else here—sons-in-law, sons or daughters, or anyone else in the city who belongs to you? Get them out of here, because we are going to destroy this place. The outcry to the LORD against its people is so great that he has sent us to destroy it" (19:12,13). It had become clear to the angels that there were not even ten godly inhabitants in that sinful city.

While relatives remain individuals with free will, the impact of godly family members (especially heads of the households) can be efficacious. The apostle Paul alludes to this effect in I Corinthians 7:14. "For the unbelieving husband has been sanctified through his wife, and the unbelieving wife has been sanctified through her believing husband. Otherwise your children would be unclean, but as it is, they are holy." What an incredible responsibility we carry for our families. Though somewhat diminished by his wandering ways, Lot's faith in God would save those who belonged to him from the terrible judgment about to fall on the unrepentant citizens of Sodom.

In response to the angels' charge to get anyone who belonged to him out of the city, Lot attempted to warn the two men of Sodom to whom his two daughters were betrothed. The account says that he *"went out"* and spoke with them. Clearly, they were not in Lot's house at the time. That detail creates a question about the status of those men. As quoted earlier, verse 4 tells us that "...all the men from every part of the city of Sodom—both young and old—surrounded the house." Does that mean this pair were also among those demanding to sexually assault Lot's guests? What kind of men had this righteous father chosen for his daughters to wed?

The reaction of Lot's future sons-in-law to his warning raises even more questions. "He said, 'Hurry and get out of this place, because the LORD is about to destroy the city!' But his sons-in-law thought he was joking" (19:14). Why didn't they take such an urgent admonition seriously?

Were they so averse to matters of faith that they automatically dismissed out of hand the possibility of divine judgment? Were carnal pleasure and material prosperity the only things in life that mattered? Had Lot never before spoken to them of spiritual matters? Or was his witness so feeble that it made no real impact, perhaps the witness of his words being too inconsistent with that of his lifestyle? Maybe their reaction resulted from the combination of Lot's ineffective testimony and their irredeemable hardened sinful hearts. We don't know for sure. Whatever the source of their unbelief, they foolishly chose to stay in the condemned city.

Time was quickly passing and Lot himself was slow to escape with his family. As dawn approached, his rescuers urged him to get moving lest he and his household perish with their wicked neighbors. "When he hesitated, the men grasped his hand and the hands of his wife and of his two daughters and led them safely out of the city, for the LORD was merciful to them" (19:16). What was the root of his hesitancy? I believe it was Lot's unwise attachment to the affluence of the region he'd chosen to call home. That little of the goods he'd possessed in Sodom could be taken with them is made clear by the fact that one of each of their hands were engaged in grasping the hands of their heavenly visitors.

The angels pressed him to "flee to the mountains or you will be swept away" (19:17). Once again Lot wavered.

"But Lot said to them, 'No, my lords, please! Your servant has found favor in your eyes, and you have shown great kindness to me in sparing my life. But I can't flee to the mountains; this disaster will overtake me, and I'll die'" (19:18,19). Apparently Lot did not fully trust in God's Word given through His heavenly messengers.

He decided that his own reasoning was better than the Lord's. God said "flee to the mountains." Lot reasoned that if he did what God said, "this disaster will overtake me and I'll die." Human unbelief exalts itself over the Word of the Lord.

Lot had his own idea. "Look, here is a town near enough to run to, and it is small. Let me flee to it—it is very small, isn't it? Then my life will be spared'" (19:20). From the beginning of the divine warning he'd disrespected God's timing and moved at his own pace. Now he decided that a nearby town was a safer destination than that advised by the angels.

It's interesting to note that Lot remarked that this community was small... *very* small. The implication is that being small, it was unlikely to be so wicked as were Sodom and Gomorrah. This rationale is consistent with the observation that sin and crime tend to be more pervasive in larger communities. Fallen human nature is such that when a greater number of people settle in one limited area, wickedness tends to multiply. It's not that people in larger cities are inherently corrupt. It's that all of our carnal natures are, and that somehow the more of us who live in close proximity, it seems the more we're encouraged to commit the evil deeds arising from our lower nature. And tightly compacted populations can feel more social pressure to conform to a common culture than those widely dispersed in rural areas.

The angels granted Lot's request to escape to the nearby town, but their response included a further statement which indicated how unnecessary were Lot's fears of being overtaken by the disaster about to fall upon the city he was leaving. "But flee there quickly, *because I cannot do anything until you reach it*" (19:22). They had been commanded by God not to allow judgment to start until Lot and his family had fully escaped. There had been no need for him to alter his escape route for fear of getting caught in the destruction.

The sun had risen by the time the family had reached the little hamlet of Zoar, and the rain of burning sulfur began. Divine judgment upon Sodom and Gomorrah engulfed the entire plain of the Jordan, destroying not only the unrepentant grossly sinful people in those wicked cities, but all the vegetation throughout the valley.

The brief description of that event ended with a heartbreaking postscript. "But Lot's wife looked back, and she became a pillar of salt" (19:26). The family had been plainly told *not* to look back (19:17). Lot's attachment to Sodom and it's luxurious lifestyle had caused him to linger longer than he should have. Yet he ultimately obeyed the order to depart. His wife's devotion to the culture of that city was so strong that it compelled her to disobey the command not to look back. It cost her her life!

Jesus likened the circumstances of this story to those of His coming return to earth. "It was the same in the days of Lot. People were eating and drinking, buying and selling, planting and building. But the day Lot left Sodom, fire and sulfur rained down from heaven and destroyed them all. It will be just like this on the day the Son of Man is revealed. On that day no one who is on the roof of his house, with his goods inside, should go down to get them. Likewise, no one in the field should go back for anything. Remember Lot's wife! Whoever tries to keep his life will lose it, and whoever loses his life will preserve it" (Luke 17:28-33).

Lot's faith in God had enabled his family to evade the judgment that fell upon a profane people, yet his wayward desires for worldly prosperity and pleasures had exposed them to the powerful negative influence of that culture. His wife had safely exited the city in body, but its values had invaded her soul and conquered it. As the high priest of his home, Lot should have counted the potential cost before making strange bedfellows with a godless society.

The transformation of Lot's wife into a pillar of salt may not have been instantaneous. Scholars have reasoned that after she died as a result of her disobedience, her body was encrusted with the salt which permeates the region around the Dead (Salt) Sea. To this day, objects near that body of water are often coated with salt in the same manner.

In an epilogue of sorts to the account of Abraham's earlier intercession for Sodom recorded in the latter half of Genesis chapter 18, Scripture now tells of his observations on the morning after. "Early the next morning Abraham got up and returned to the place where he had stood before the LORD. He looked down toward Sodom and Gomorrah, toward all the land of the plain, and he saw dense smoke rising from the land, like smoke from a furnace. So when God destroyed the cities of the plain, he remembered Abraham, and he brought Lot out of the catastrophe that overthrew the cities where Lot had lived" (19:27-29).

The ten righteous inhabitants necessary for the sparing of Sodom did not exist, but in response to Abraham's prayers, Lot and his daughters had escaped judgment. I call your attention to the fact that Scripture does not say that *God remembered Lot* and rescued him. It declares that *He remembered Abraham* and saved Lot. We've established that both men were imperfect. However, in his imperfection Abraham was still a man of prayer. We know he'd interceded for the inhabitants of Sodom, including his nephew, Lot, and his family. There's no record of Lot interceding for his fellow citizens. Although the city still had to be destroyed for its unrelenting wickedness, Lot was spared in large part because of Abraham's prayers.

The foundation of every truly fruitful life is the Word of God and prayer. Abraham's spiritual intervention on behalf of Lot and Sodom had begun with God speaking to him. We read of how God decided to tell his chosen servant about his determination to judge unrepentant sin, and that He had come down to determine how bad the sin of Sodom and Gomorrah really was. In response to that word, Abraham prayed to the Lord for mercy for the citizens of those wicked cities, particularly Sodom, where Lot dwelt. Lot's rescue had begun with that divine/human interaction between Yahweh and Abraham: the Word of God and prayer. This kind of fellowship between the Creator and human beings produces godly fruit.

With verse 30, Scripture turns the focus back to Lot's wanderings and affords us the last details the Old Testament offers concerning his life. It begins with word of his ultimate post-Sodom relocation. "Lot and his two daughters left Zoar and settled in the mountains, for he was afraid to stay in Zoar. He and his two daughters lived in a cave." Talk about a riches to rags story!

His motive for the move was fear. We're not told the cause of that fear. However long Lot and his daughters had remained in Zoar, it may have been long enough for him to think through his initial unwillingness to follow the Lord's direction to flee to the mountains. He had been distrustful and disobedient, and was worthy of divine discipline. His fear could have been of such chastisement, bringing him to the place where he belatedly yielded to God's earlier command.

Maybe his fear stemmed from the kind of neighbors he discovered in Zoar. Perhaps they blamed him for the destruction of the nearby cities. They could have been angry at him, even threatening violent retribution. Or maybe he learned that the people in this little village were not as innocent as he first thought, and was now afraid that this community would soon fall victim to the same kind of judgment which befell Sodom and Gomorrah. When we choose our own paths instead of the Lord's will, we risk trouble of our own making.

Why didn't Lot choose to return to the company of his godly uncle? The circumstances that led to their separation were now totally behind him. His wealth was gone. The large flocks and herds that had led to quarreling among his and Abraham's herdsmen were nowhere to be found. He needed the wise and righteous sway of his elder in the Lord. Lot could have rejoined the family. Instead he essentially became a hermit, living in a cave with his offspring.

We're saddened as we witness the decline of Lot

and his daughters. It began earlier with the decision he made to be willing to keep company with a wicked culture in order to pursue greater material prosperity. He had gradually moved further away from the holy influence of Abraham into the profane environment of an intensely sinful society. Now in the aftermath of the destruction of Sodom, he had lost his worldly goods and descended into destitute isolation. Yet Lot's slide had still not reached its bottom. Verse 31 tragically ushers us into the setting of an even lower moral level to which his life had sunk.

The final chapter of Lot's life is indeed a sad one. The story begins with a conversation between his daughters. The eldest one expressed concern about the future of the family. "One day the older daughter said to the younger, 'Our father is old, and there is no man around here to lie with us, as is the custom all over the earth. Let's get our father to drink wine and then lie with him and preserve our family line through our father'" (19:31,32). Why did they discuss the dilemma only between themselves? Why didn't they address the issue to their father, asking him to consider properly rectifying it?

The senior daughter's proposed means of carrying on the family name was certainly immoral, but the responsibility for such sinful activity did not rest solely upon these two young women. Lot had failed to provide godly mates for his children. Back in Sodom he'd either chosen the unbelieving grooms for them, or allowed his daughters to do so on their own. Those evil men had died in divine judgment.

Now in his self-imposed isolation, Lot had made no effort to find his children appropriate mates. Abraham would eventually send his servant on a long and purposeful journey to find a God-fearing wife for his son, Isaac. But Lot had not bothered to seek honorable marriage partners for his girls. Thus he bore much accountability for the sexual sins which followed. Once more we see how our unhealthy choices can negatively affect those around us, especially the next generation.

But Lot's guilt in the matter was not limited to his failure to carry out his parental duties by providing suitable husbands for his daughters. Verses 33 through 36 record how they effectively carried out their perverse scheme by getting their father drunk... so heavily intoxicated that he wasn't even aware of the incestuous activities in which he himself was involved! This was the same man who, regarding his earlier days, had been referred to by the apostle Peter as a "righteous soul." We all face the risk of this same kind of spiritual decline when we begin to compromise with the culture of this fallen world.

The Genesis biography of Lot ends with verses 36 through 38. They affirm the fulfillment of his daughters' plans, then point us toward the fate of his future descendants. "So both of Lot's daughters became pregnant by their father. The older daughter had a son, and she named him Moab; he is the father of the Moabites of today. The younger daughter also had a son, and she named him Ben-Ammi; he is the father of the Ammonites of today." *Moab* appears to be derived from the Hebrew word for *from father. Ben-Ammi* means *son of my people.*

These two clans, whose ancestor, Lot, had once been a close godly relative of the father of the Israelites, eventually became the enemies of the Jews. Centuries after the death of the patriarchs, they attempted to stop

God's chosen people from entering the land the Lord had promised to Abraham and his descendants. For this reason God ultimately warned Israel not to befriend them.

"No one born of a forbidden marriage nor any of his descendants may enter the assembly of the LORD, even down to the tenth generation. No Ammonite or Moabite or any of his descendants may enter the assembly of the LORD, even down to the tenth generation. For they did not come to meet you with bread and water on your way when you came out of Egypt, and they hired Balaam son of Beor from Pethor in Aram Naharaim to pronounce a curse on you. However, the LORD your God would not listen to Balaam but turned the curse into a blessing for you, because the LORD your God loves you. Do not seek a treaty of friendship with them as long as you live" (Deuteronomy 23:2-6).

Still, even many centuries after the Balaam affair, the Psalmist records the fact that Lot's descendants continued to be allied with the enemies of the Israelites (see Psalm 83:5-8). How unfortunate that the spiritual driftings of one person can adversely impact an extended family for generations. This is, however, a fact of life in this sinful world.

Overall, throughout their history the Ammonites and Moabites continued in idolatry, wickedness, and enmity against the Lord and His chosen people. Eventually, King David had to go to battle against them because of their continued opposition to the Israelites. He eventually defeated and subdued these enemies of God. Much later, the prophet Ezekiel foretold their final and complete destruction (see Ezekiel 25:1-11). What a sad ending for the descendants of a righteous man who wandered from the ways of the Lord.

Yet that widespread ethnic backsliding did not lock all of Lot's offspring into an unalterable tragic fate. The book of Ruth is a glorious historic tale of one Moabite woman who not only found her way into fellowship with Yahweh and His people Israel, but was honored by God to be archived into the lineage of the Messiah, Jesus Himself (see Matthew 1:5). God's love and mercy are so powerful that anyone can be reconciled to Him through personal repentance and faith!

What about Lot himself? His biography in the opening volume of God's Word ends on a discordant note. He is one half of the pair of righteous men who headline this book you're reading. Both were clearly far from perfect. Still the contrast between the stories of these men is notable.

Abraham was the one who responded directly to the command of the Lord to leave home and go to an unknown land. Lot accompanied him, but there's no indication that he walked in the kind of intimate communion with the Creator which was so foundational to Abraham's earthly pilgrimage. Throughout his journeys Abraham built altars to worship Yahweh. There's no record of Lot ever doing so. Worship is at the core of our relationship with God.

Abraham was God's friend, and never turned his heart away in spite of his personal failures. Each time he sinned he repented, got back up, and continued his pursuit of righteousness. Lot's desire for God was gradually displaced by a love for the things of the world. He compromised with the sinful culture around him to the point where he became a friend of this world. It ultimately cost him his possessions, and in more ways than one, his family. Most pitifully, it cost him the plans the Lord had for a blessed God-filled life for him.

Abraham's faithfulness afforded him a powerful position of sacred influence upon his descendants... both his physical (Israel) and his spiritual (Christians) posterity. The passing of thousands of years has not diminished its affect. His life story still challenges and encourages us. Lot, in spite of his early years of fellowship with his God and his uncle, is remembered predominately for his wanderings from the Lord, and into accommodation with a corrupt society. Among Sodom's citizenry he did not lead a single soul to faith in Yahweh!

In the end, we may ask: "Did Lot lose his own faith in the Lord? Did he as a result pay the ultimate price? Did he lose his salvation?" I don't see in Scripture a distinct answer to those questions. I'm inclined though, to believe that Lot held to his faith, as weak as it may have become, and in God's mercy he remained in the fold. But I can't say that with certainty. Whatever the final verdict, he paid a heavy toll in this life for his wanderings, and risked losing his faith in the Lord, and the eternal life in heaven which is the greatest benefit of that faith!

So now we've finished reviewing the biblical accounts of the two righteous men and the two wicked cities which are the primary subject of this book. We've learned lessons from them that can and should be practiced in our individual lives as believers. Those lessons also need to be employed in earthly societies for the benefit of all. In our final two chapters we'll expand particularly upon the critical application of those lessons to two communal entities whom I'm convinced the Almighty cares about deeply: the American nation and the American church. If you truly believe He loves us, then flip the page and open up your heart and mind.

Chapter 5

The Ancient Paradigm Recurs, Part 1

(The American Nation)

Scripture does not share the account of Abraham and Lot and Sodom and Gomorrah simply to entertain us with an intriguing story. The better part of 15 chapters in the first book of the Bible are absorbed in conveying these remarkable annals in order to teach future generations how to truly live life in rewarding fellowship with our Creator. The Old Testament records of the history of God's people are meant to show us what to pursue, and what to avoid. In the midst of a reference to Israel's fall into idolatry, Paul affirms this fact in I Corinthians 10:6: "Now these things occurred as examples to keep us from setting our hearts on evil things as they did."

The divine truths discovered through our prayerful study of the events covered in the biblical story of two righteous men and two wicked cities, should be applied to every era of human existence. We must especially acknowledge that even today there exist parallels to this biography of two individuals and two communities. We've already occasionally touched on the application of these truths to us in previous chapters, but in this chapter we'll probe these issues in greater depth and detail as they apply to our country as well.

God relates to human beings in their various units such as: individuals, families, communities, and nations. Sodom and Gomorrah are examples of those societies who, whether ignorantly or knowingly, have chosen the way of Satan and thus come under the dominion of a world system that has rejected God's Kingdom. Abraham and Lot on the other hand, represent not only two general types of Christian individuals, but two kinds of Christian families and spiritual brotherhoods... even two categories of nations.

It's critical that we identify the current entities which correspond to those in the story we've just examined. That's the only way to learn how to become the people the Lord wants us to be, and to have a godly impact in 21st century societies. Otherwise we may choose the wrong paths, and when we do so, we can negatively impact others around us as well.

Everything good or evil that occurs in the human realm begins with individuals. From there it spreads to families, communities, and nations. As we pointed out in chapter one of this book, the inception of the dark side of this process is to be observed in the account of the fall of man in the Garden of Eden. Eve decided to buy into the philosophy espoused by Satan, who subsequently became the god of this world. From there it spread to Adam, then to the children of the first couple, and eventually to all their offspring in all the generations which followed.

While each person has always had the God-given gift of free will by which (through faith and repentance) to reverse this sinful trend, the capacity of peer pressure from the unredeemed to persuade individuals otherwise, remains powerful. So we must decide whether to yield to the influence of the seductive false propaganda of this fallen world, or instead respond to the spiritual appeal in the righteous truths of a loving, holy God. The choices we make will not only determine the course of our own lives, they can encourage others around us to follow that same road, whether it's the one that leads to heaven, or the one that leads to hell.

In this chapter we aim to recognize that the legacies of Abraham and Lot, and Sodom and Gomorrah are still at work in our world many centuries later. Once again I'm reminded of the old saying we mentioned in chapter 3: "History repeats itself." This fact is pronounced in Scripture. "Whatever has already been, and what will be has been before; and God will call the past to account" (Ecclesiastes 3:15).

If we honestly accept this truth, we need to consider how we, and those around us, may fit into the ancient paradigm of this revealing story we've just studied. Then we need to decide whose legacy we personally will emulate. Will we follow the path of Abraham the faithful, or Lot the wanderer? Will we accommodate the prevailing ungodly culture, or stand strong against sin, while loving sinners? Will we be a friend of God, or a friend of the perverse world system? Our individual life choices will have broad potential influence, reaching from our family, to our church, to our community… even to our nation!

In dealing with the above questions, we'll primarily take a look at two critical modern entities dramatically affected by our individual choices in these matters: *the American nation and the American church.* We'll consider the origins, and current broad decline, of these two powerful entities. We'll also determine what we as individual believers should do to help reverse their tragic downward trends. May God use His precious Holy Spirit to anoint the vital truths of His Word in speaking to our hearts!

In this chapter we'll deal with the decline of America the nation. The United States of my childhood (1950's) was a very different country than the one in which we live today. Until prayer in public schools was ruled against by the Supreme Court while I was in junior high, I remember each school day beginning with the teacher standing at the front of the classroom reading a passage of Scripture aloud, then leading us students in a recitation of the Lord's Prayer. Finally we all stood and pledged allegiance to the flag of "one nation under God." Such public religious and patriotic practices were common at the time.

Back then the vast majority of citizens at least had respect for Christian values, even if they themselves were not believers. While significant levels of immorality existed, such behavior was not as widespread as it is now. And unlike in contemporary America, sinful lifestyles were not broadly endorsed as acceptable, and certainly not publicly promoted as they often are today! The United States of 2020 bears little resemblance to the nation in which I grew up. My heart often breaks as I watch how our country continues to move further and further away from our historical Christian foundations.

I've pretty much understood all of my adult life that once a people reject God and His Word, morality is eventually abandoned as well. Many years ago, however, the Lord spoke to my heart and told me that once morality is gone, common sense isn't far behind. Sadly, America has reached that point where common sense is virtually as much a thing of the past as is morality in the prevailing public culture.

While the outlawing of prayer in our schools may not have been *the* decisive factor in our modern spiritual and moral decline, it clearly was a major ingredient. In his book "Original Intent," noted historian David Barton charts the disturbing downward trends of our society from that point forward. Various negative cultural consequences have exploded through the American populace since that 1963 Supreme Court ruling eliminating prayer in schools. Rates of teen pregnancy, sexually transmitted diseases, single parent households, and violent crime have skyrocketed. Meanwhile our educational system has taken a remarkable hit as SAT scores have plummeted.

Numerous subsequent Supreme Court decisions became further alarming road signs on the journey to the present immoral swamp which surrounds us. We'll take a quick look at a few of those judicial edicts a bit later.

To discover the deep seminal Christian roots of our land, however, we need to go back much further than those nearly six decades ago when America took a basic trend-setting critical turn away from our rich spiritual heritage. In highlighting our beginnings in certain paragraphs that will follow, I don't mean to suggest that this country and it's leaders were ever perfect, but I do intend to establish the fact that the United States was begun upon a godly foundation constructed by men and women who recognized the essential necessity of acknowledging the overruling authority of the Creator.

First, however, let's recognize a few of the more widespread sins which prevailed during the earlier periods of our history. These misdeeds tended to involve abuse of certain people groups. Such actions sometimes carried the weight of local, state, or national government edicts. Other times they were societal in origin. Most true Christians usually were non-participants in, even outright opponents of, these inhumane injustices. Still, just as in today's America, some believers yielded to sinful motives.

There was the poor treatment of, and at times outright atrocities against, Native Americans. Most of the early European settlers treated these tribes with respect and friendship, even introducing them to the Gospel. Yet disrespect and abuse eventually became quite pervasive. Tribes were forced out of their lands and even massacred on occasions. Although Christian missionaries sought to share the love of Jesus with native Americans, harsh treatment of them from others still prevailed. While the bulk of the atrocities were clearly wrought by Europeans against Natives, there were reverse cruelties too, as when some tribes murdered early Christian missionaries and ruthlessly slaughtered whole communities of innocent men, women, and children.

The enslavement of Africans actually began on the African continent, then primarily spread to parts of Europe, particularly England. The first African slaves arrived in North America very early, and the practice became deeply entrenched as the colonies grew. Using the fact that slavery was an accepted part of their regional culture, many professing Christians attempted to re-interpret certain passages of the Bible to wrongfully support it. Even some eventual founding fathers had become slave owners. That cruel practice continued (primarily in southern states) until the end of the Civil War. This is not to say that all, or even most, early Americans supported the institution of slavery. Some devout white Christians shared the Gospel with slaves, and some also became active abolitionists.

Unfortunately, even after slavery was outlawed, cultural racism carried on much of its awful legacy in the form of segregation, and even murderous lynchings, in large regions of the country for nearly another century. Although in more recent decades we've made much progress in reducing racism against blacks, and it no longer runs as deep and wide as it did in the past, a significant residue of it still exists in the U.S.

During the nineteenth century, abuse of certain immigrant nationalities went on at cultural and business levels, rising to governmental levels in some cases. Irish, Italian, and Chinese suffered from this type of victimization, which also turned violent on occasions. And remember the internment of Japanese Americans in WW II. What should have counted was not race, ethnicity, or national origin, but character, and the finest source of righteous character should flow from following Jesus as Lord and Savior. Racism in any form or direction should have no place in the nation which in the past has been referred to as "the melting pot of the world."

For most of my life I've had a deep sense that

despite our national shortcomings, God has ordained a special place in history for America. That sense was only strengthened as a result of my personal research and interviews with historians done in preparation for an hour-long broadcast special I produced back in the mid-1990's. Titled: "Come Home, America," it was aired on many Christian radio stations across the country at the time. In several paragraphs which follow I want to highlight just a very few of the truths I learned about our nation's beginnings.

I should preface my recounting of these facts by pointing out that most of this information has been virtually eliminated from contemporary history textbooks. In an effort to destroy any recognition of our godly spiritual heritage, such accounts now emphasize the detrimental aspects of America's story to the nearly total neglect of its beneficial aspects. As I stated, the United States and its leaders have never been perfect, but that should not prohibit us from openly acknowledging and celebrating the good which has helped make it the most powerful and prosperous nation on earth. As we learned, neither Abraham nor the nation which rose from his descendants were ever perfect either. Yet God's blessings rested upon them in response to their faith.

Let's begin our brief review of America's divine origins with a discoverer who had for centuries been considered a hero. He has more recently been almost totally villainized. Many individuals and groups have called for the repudiation of the holiday created in his honor. His name? Christopher Columbus.

Were his character and motives totally impeccable? Of course not. What human being on earth can claim that kind of flawless record? But the fact is that a primary reason for his voyage to what he expected would be parts of Asia, was to bring the Gospel message there. This effort was largely in response to the Chinese emperor's request for more information about Christianity, an appeal made to Marco Polo more than two centuries earlier.

Columbus' motivation on this matter is clearly documented in his writings. He actually considered himself a missionary. The first thing he did upon landing on North American shores in 1492, was to fall upon his knees in prayer and praise. "Oh Lord, almighty and everlasting God, by Thy Holy Word Thou hast created the heaven, and the earth, and the sea. Blessed and glorified be Thy name, and praised be Thy majesty which hath deigned to use us, Thy humble servants, that Thy holy name may be proclaimed in this second part of the earth."

In the years that followed his journeys to the distant western continents, Christian missionaries from Spain and France sought to evangelize Native Americans. A few of them paid with their lives in their labors for the Gospel. Ultimately our nation, which was eventually established in this new world Columbus sailed to, became the most active evangelistic nation in history. Coincidence? I think not. The United States has sent more Christian missionaries around the planet than any other country in history!

In 1620 a pivotal group of newcomers arrived in North America. The Pilgrims had been granted land within the territory of the "Virginia Company of Plymouth." Upon completing the very dangerous three month trek over the Atlantic Ocean, they finally disembarked upon the shores of what is now known as Cape Cod in eastern Massachusetts. Like Columbus before them, upon their arrival in America they immediately prayed. "Being thus arrived in a good harbor, and brought safe to land, they fell upon their knees, and blessed the God of heaven who had brought them over the vast and furious ocean and delivered them from all the perils and miseries thereof..." This is a direct quote from their leader William Bradford's record of their history.

The Pilgrims are generally said to have come here seeking freedom of worship. That's not entirely true. Upon leaving England to escape persecution from the state church, they'd migrated to Holland and lived in religious liberty there for more than a decade. But their sense of a higher calling involved more than just worshiping together. Their famous "Mayflower Compact" made clear the greater reason why they sailed across the Atlantic.

In setting forth the corporate covenant upon which they would establish their form of colonial self-government, the Mayflower Compact first defined the primary purpose of the Pilgrims' venture. It clarifies their objectives: "Having undertaken, *for the glory of God and advancement of the Christian Faith* and honor of our King and country, a voyage to plant the first colony in the northern parts of Virginia..." Their overriding purpose in coming to America was to glorify God and spread His Gospel. The Pilgrims even felt specifically called of the Lord to propagate that Gospel among the Indians.

The Mayflower Compact is traditionally considered to be the foundation upon which the U.S. Constitution was built some 168 years later. This is an important element in seeing the hand of God at work in the establishment of our nation. The biblical perspective on proper government continued to be prominent here, as other groups sailed to this fledgling republic.

The Pilgrims' spiritual cousins, the Puritans, arrived in the new world some twenty years later. They also established a Bible-based form of democracy, as New England developed into an admirable model of a Christian commonwealth. Sadly, as is often the case over the course of human history, many in colonial America drifted from its God-honoring roots. In speaking of the spiritual decline he observed among his own people, second generation Puritan preacher Cotton Mather put it this way: "Religion begat prosperity, and the daughter devoured the mother!"

Thankfully, there were enough Christians seeking the Lord for revival, that the Almighty sent His Spirit and His servant to create a powerful move of God that became known as "The First Great Awakening." The primary leader of that movement was a British preacher named George Whitefield. His ministry from Maine to Georgia did not just bring lost souls to Christ, it tended to bring unity to a largely divided American Christianity, and a widely fragmented set of American colonies.

This mighty move of God helped prepare the way for the emergence of a historically unique nation. With the most significant exception of aforementioned slavery in the southern colonies, we were emerging as a self-governing democracy based upon the equality of all men. This concept of "government of the people, by the people, and for the people" had been expressed by John Wycliffe long before President Lincoln spoke it in his Gettysburg address. Wycliffe, who was the father of the English protestant reformation, saw this governmental concept as a truth taught by the Bible.

There is so much throughout American history which renders evidence of God's calling upon us, and the blessings that have flowed when we've acted in obedience to that calling. As we move forward in succinctly reviewing that history, let's next do a concise examination of the era of its founding.

Although the North American British colonies were still under the rule of the English monarchy, they had been allowed a large measure of self-determination. As the crown steadily eroded their God-ordained liberty, however, our founding fathers came to a momentous decision. Unable to negotiate a lifting of oppressive laws from the mother country, they determined that it was time for America to become its own sovereign nation under the Creator. At issue was not simply taxation without representation. It was their commitment to the kind of freedom that came from recognizing God as the supreme ruler.

Upon the completion of the Declaration of Independence on July 4, 1776, one of the leading founding fathers, Sam Adams, stood to his feet asserting what he saw as the essence of the reasoning behind this groundbreaking proclamation. "We have this day restored the Sovereign to Whom alone men ought to be obedient. From the rising to the setting sun may His Kingdom come!"

Sam Adams was the cousin of America's second president: John Adams. Both were devout Christians. The former is not as well known as his presidential relative, but he was the early leader and spokesman for the movement for independence. Recognizing his pivotal role in organizing numerous critical aspects of this movement, the British began to refer to the war for independence as "Mr. Adams' war." And this man clearly viewed the recognition of the sovereignty of the God of the Bible as a central issue!

Sam Adams was not alone in that spiritual perspective. Out of 270 founding fathers of our country, only about a dozen were *not* Christians. The rest were openly professing and practicing Christians. But in most public school American history textbooks today, our founding fathers are almost universally portrayed as atheists, agnostics, and deists. If that were true, then how do we explain that out of their ranks 121 Bible societies were formed? In addition, they established numerous missionary and gospel tract societies. There's obviously something wrong with the picture presented in such commonly used secular historical accounts.

The man who has been universally acknowledged as *the father of our country* was one of the most devout among our Christian founders. General George Washington was the supreme leader of the American army during the Revolutionary War. Numerous personal witnesses proclaimed his godly character and prayerful devotion to the Lord. During the war his abundant correspondence repeatedly credited divine providence for amazing interventions on our nation's behalf. Later, as the first President of the United States he firmly declared: "It is impossible to rightly govern... without God and the Bible."

There is much more overwhelming historically documented evidence of the Christian roots of our nation than I have time to list in this book. I could easily share many direct quotes from our founding fathers which undeniably support this truth. And it was not only the clearly Christian founders who publicly acknowledged it, even numerous leaders who were not practicing believers understood the good and powerful effect of Christianity upon our nation. I cite just one such example. "History will afford frequent opportunities of showing the necessity of a public religion... and the Excellency of the Christian religion above all others, ancient or modern" - Benjamin Franklin.

Despite some ups and downs, the beneficial sway of the Scriptures continued in the decades following our independence from England. Alexis de Tocqueville, a French diplomat, political scientist, and historian, was sent to our burgeoning country in 1831 by the French government. Initially, his purpose was primarily to study the uniqueness of American prisons, but his extensive travels here led him to discover a much broader panorama of remarkable things. Notably, he observed the pervasive influence of Christianity upon this nation.

He recorded the following observation in his classic work: *Democracy in America*. "There is no country in the whole world in which the Christian religion retains a greater influence over the souls of men than in America. And there can be no greater proof of its utility and its conformity to human nature than that it's influence is most powerfully felt over the most enlightened and free nation on earth."

This prevailing prominence of Bible values in the history of the United States extends far beyond those early years. Even the U. S. Supreme Court described America as a "Christian nation" in four different legal rulings over a nearly 90 year period from 1844 through 1931. However, if after reading all of the above cited evidence you still have any doubts about this country's Christian origins,

I would recommend in particular that you read some of the authoritative books on the matter written by diligent historians such as David Barton, and co-authors Peter Marshall and David Manuel.

America is a prime example of a country that has experienced blessings and prosperity because of the widespread influence of Scriptural principles, yet it doesn't stand alone in history. In 2007, Youth with a Mission founder, Loren Cunningham, published a work which chronicles the stories of other governments powerfully and positively affected by the Bible. *The Book that Transforms Nations* cites numerous dominions changed for the good through the spread of God's Word over the centuries. Among them are India, the Netherlands, Norway, South Korea, Germany, and even little Pitcairn Island in the vast Pacific Ocean. Sadly, like contemporary America, many of these people have wandered away from such beneficial spiritual and ethical moorings.

While in that regard our country has much in common with those listed above, I've sensed in many ways an even greater parallel between the nation of *Israel* and our own. I believe both are in some dimension a *chosen people*. I'm not alone in this belief in a divine destiny for America. Twenty years ago I had the privilege of interviewing a former high ranking Israeli government official. Eli Mizrachi had served under more than one of that nation's prime ministers. He told me he felt strongly that there was a link between Jerusalem and Washington D. C... an affinity between Israel and America.

As Israel was preparing to celebrate in 1996 the 3,000[th] anniversary of David's conquest of Jerusalem, Eli wanted to find out who the first true Americans were to enter

Jerusalem. He was not looking for those who traveled to the holy city while living here when America was still a British colony, but only the first who did so after it had become its own sovereign nation. His research determined that those Americans were two young Christian missionaries who went there in 1819 to preach the Gospel of Christ to the Jewish people! To me this is another sign that our country was assigned a mission from God. Eli uncovered historical documents (correspondence, journals, diaries, accounts, etc.) which enabled him to chronicle their story in a wonderful book he titled: "Two Americans within the Gates." It's an insightful and inspiring read. I highly recommend it.

Just as Israel periodically forsook their calling from God, so has the United States. While America has been profoundly shaped by Christianity, once again I don't mean to suggest that it or its leaders have ever been without faults and failures. Still, its goodness has stood above that of the vast majority of other countries through most of its two and a half centuries of existence. Sadly, now it's character is rampant with widespread iniquity and violence, often fed by such feelings as selfishness, anger, and hatred. In my seven decades of life here, watching our spiritual and moral decline has brought much grief to my heart. Of even greater concern though, is the grief it has brought to the heart of God.

What has been the source of this decline? What has been the mechanism? The author of our corruption has been the devil himself! This enemy of God and human souls is behind all wickedness on the planet. Satan entices individuals to sinful rebellion against the Lord through appealing to their base desires such as pride, greed, perverse pleasures, self-indulgent anger, and vengeance. Then he uses them and their social institutions as pawns to propagate his lies and his evil agenda.

This has been the enemy's modus operandi since the beginning of time. As we noted earlier, he persuaded Adam and Eve to reject *the Creator's* truths and commands, and believe *his* deceptions. From that point on the devil's lies spread so widely among mankind that it reached the point where in Noah's day "...every inclination of the thoughts of his *[humanity's]* heart was only evil all the time." (Genesis 6:5)

Over the course of time numerous Satanic falsehoods began to take hold in the minds of people in our now independent country. They started with what might be considered less extreme beliefs like deism and agnosticism. These morphed into atheism and stronger anti-God attitudes. At first these errors were espoused by a relative few. Little by little over time the number of adherents to such erroneous philosophies increased, and even more godless thinking unfurled across the nation.

Two of these morally cancerous arguments arose in England and traversed the Atlantic to the U.S. during the 19th century. Charles Darwin proposed that human beings and all other life forms were not created by a divine being, but had over millions of years somehow evolved from non-living matter. Although there was, and still is, no true scientific proof of such a theory, it gained a foothold and eventually became considered as established scientific fact. The theory of evolution was akin to another false belief system of that era: secularism. Englishman George Holyoake was instrumental in defining and establishing this philosophy. It was a precursor to secular humanism, which purports that humanity is capable of morality and self-fulfillment without belief in God. Evolution and secularism began to peck away at America's biblical foundations.

In the 20th century even more errant movements arose, shifting our culture further from its once prevailing Christian origins. The meaning of the first amendment of the Constitution has been effectively distorted from "freedom *of* religion" to "freedom *from* religion" as the Supreme Court removed prayer from the schools in 1963 as we previously mentioned. By that same Supreme Court, "person-hood" was stripped from children in their mother's wombs in 1973, and they came to be described as "fetal tissue." Through a distortion of the Constitution's "right to privacy," abortion was made legal without such a law ever being passed by congress. Sexual promiscuity outside of marriage, and even other sexual perversions (particularly homosexuality), became more commonly accepted, and then vested with special legal rights.

Now in the 21st century additional societal walls against sexual wickedness were torn down by the U.S. Supreme Court as in 2015 homosexuals were given the right to same-sex marriage. People... *including young children...* are now being told that they can be any gender they want, despite what sex they were physically at birth. Hormonal and surgical procedures attempting to change the gender of not only adults, but the aforementioned young children, are considered by a significant segment of society to be a personal right.

Christians who hold to convictions differing from these positions are considered "haters," and in some areas are being denied the right to fully live out their personal beliefs. If wayward movements continue their current direction, things are only going to get worse. America is already *post-Christian*, and may become totally *anti-Christian*.

Let's consider for a moment the societal institutions the devil, and the human proponents of such anti-biblical philosophies, have used to disseminate these and other falsehoods to the point where so many have accepted them as facts. First, let me say that *individuals* can certainly wield influence, but with lesser impact. Human *institutions* though, have a broader reach, and tend to carry a greater sense of authority. Thus we recognize the critical role of these institutions in the shaping of a society.

The three primary institutions used by opponents of Christian truths and morals are: education, media, and government. They've infiltrated, largely taken control of, and used these institutions to erase the biblical principles upon which America was built, and replace them with destructive shameful values. The impact of these institutions on popular culture have in a sense mimicked that of the cities of Sodom and Gomorrah upon Lot and his family. This transformation of our country's culture was done gradually, rendering the process less perceptible and, thus over the course of time, progressively more acceptable by the general public. Rather than one initial in-your-face complete repudiation of traditional cultural mores, the step by step method worked a more effective indoctrination of the American people.

God used the Apostle Paul to warn the first century Corinthians against this kind of spiritually and morally destructive influence. In I Corinthians 15:33,34 he advises: "Do not be misled: 'Bad company corrupts good character.' Come back to your senses as you ought, and stop sinning; for there are some who are ignorant of God—I say this to your shame." Sadly, once Christian America has allowed the failed philosophies of an ungodly culture to shrewdly lead us away from our roots in the Bible.

I believe education was the initial arena where the enemies of God went to work in their efforts to reconstruct the national mindset. As with the theory of evolution, the philosophy of secular humanism has wormed its way into our educational system. Although both public and higher education in this country were initially created by Christians and based upon biblical values, our schools have yielded to the aggressive influence of secular humanism. We would do well to return to the view of schooling espoused by the man who created the first American English dictionary in 1828, and is considered to be the *original* father of American education: Noah Webster. He declared that "education is useless without the Bible. The Bible was America's basic text book in all fields. God's Word, contained in the Bible, has furnished all necessary rules to direct our conduct."

Sadly, considered by most contemporary educators to be the father of *modern* American education, atheist and Marxist socialist John Dewey was a prime mover in this takeover. In the early 20th century he commenced his efforts to reconstruct our schools by authoring the influential book: *Democracy and Education*. He and his comrades later devised a plan to transform our schools and their curriculum. He co-authored and signed the *Humanist Manifesto*. Dewey became the first honorary president of the NEA (National Education Association).

From their positions of influence, he and others of his ilk were able to begin to carry out their plans. Under their tutelage our educational institutions have not only pushed the Creator out of the curriculum, they've pushed scholastic scores steadily downhill.

The disappearance of any record of the pivotal role of Christianity in the establishment and development of the United States in current social studies textbooks, is the result of the actions of people like Dewey. This coincides with communist socialistic goals. Co-founder of communism (along with Friederich Engels) Karl Marx once said that: "The first battlefield is the rewriting of history."

George Orwell wrote a famous novel commonly referred to under the shortened title: *1984.* Penned in 1949, and describing a fictional society in existence some three and a half decades later, he wrote of a frightening future world. "Every record has been destroyed or falsified, every book rewritten, every picture has been repainted, every statue and street building has been renamed, every date has been altered. And the process is continuing day by day and minute by minute. History has stopped. Nothing exists except an endless present in which the Party is always right." Sounds hauntingly familiar doesn't it?

Later John Dewey disciple John J. Dunphy wrote in his renowned 1983 essay, *The Humanist*: "The battle for humankind's future must be waged and won in the public school classroom by teachers who correctly perceive their role as the proselytizers of a new faith: A religion of humanity – utilizing a classroom instead of a pulpit to carry humanist values into wherever they teach. The classroom must and will become an arena of conflict between the old and the new – the rotting corpse of Christianity, together with its adjacent evils and misery, and the new faith of humanism."

It's difficult even for those youth reared in Christian homes and attending Bible teaching churches to resist the tide of tainted education and peer pressure washing over them five days a week in America's public schools. The effect has been to gradually change the face of our country over the span of nearly a century. "One nation under God" has in large part become "a nation against God." The devil knows what he's doing. It behooves us as believers to also know what he's doing. In II Corinthians 2:11 Paul advises the church in that ancient city that the corrective actions he'd taken in regard to a problem there, were done "...in order that Satan might not outwit us. For we are not unaware of his schemes."

As perverted beliefs have worked their way from schools into the popular culture at large, media news accounts and entertainment productions have begun to not only *reflect* those godless values, but eventually to militantly *promote* them. The instruments of media have grown to include not only print, radio, television, and movies, but numerous internet social sites available through numerous types of digital technology.

True news reporting is meant to be unbiased and based upon real events. In the early 1980's I was trained in broadcast journalism using the prevailing standard college textbook on the subject. I was taught that such reporting was to be constructed and delivered objectively. If personal bias entered into the work it ceased to be *news casting*, and became *editorializing*. The two were to be distinctively separated. As a radio news reporter, anchor, and later as a news director, I stuck to those rules. How much such journalism has changed in the decades since! Its influence had been widely corrupted for cultural and political purposes. It frequently is not only prejudicial in its presentation, but dispenses misinformation either intentionally or through sloppy journalism.

The entertainment industry has also evolved in a negative manner. In days gone by it was normally used in an enjoyable way to bring joy, or inspire good things. We would often expect to discover the moral of the story, song, etc. Nowadays they often foster immorality, self-centeredness, greed, anger, violence, and other detrimental motivations. In the process many actors, musicians, athletes, and others have become celebrity gods of a sort. Entertainment has regularly become a form of idolatry.

Through motion picture, television, radio, printed materials, internet, and other forms of digital media, it has the power to influence hundreds of millions. The reach of contemporary media is far-ranging and pervasive. They frequently exalt devilish standards over godly ones, sensual pleasure-seeking over righteous conduct, and material riches over heavenly treasure. Everywhere we turn our eyes and ears they often push a secular humanistic view of life... sometimes subtly, sometimes blatantly. If you dare to disagree, you're slandered as a hick, a bigot... even a *hater.* They make it uncomfortable or even shameful for you to dissent.

Their spell is cast not only over those who consume their productions, but those who are involved in the creation of their productions. Over the last few decades we've witnessed numerous professional musicians, actors, and athletes who started out openly professing their faith in Christ, subsequently turn from their God fearing backgrounds to godless lifestyles, sometimes even publicly renouncing their faith. The industry's peer pressure and temptations to sin have led such once wholesome entertainers away from the Lord.

Knowingly or unwittingly, it seems most media leaders have become the enemies of God. Whether they believe they're promoting true justice for the common good, or actually are arrogantly seeking personal power and total authority and control over others, the end result is the same. America is being directed away from it's historical Christian roots and into an atheistic socialist mindset. The values which allowed this nation to receive the abundant blessings of God are being abandoned.

Once again, I'm not suggesting that the United States has ever been perfect. Other than Jesus Christ, there has not been a flawless *human being* on the planet since the fall of man in the Garden of Eden... let alone a flawless *society*. Yet based upon real history there's no question that despite our defects, we've been one of the most God-fearing nations ever. We should not allow that history to be so easily undone.

Some in the politically correct crowd choose to focus on both real and imagined wrongs in America, while essentially denying any virtues. They shame those who dare to speak proudly and affectionately of our nation. Patriotism is considered the expression of the ignorant, racist, and oppressive elite. But I believe that beyond our country's shortcomings is much that is good. If any earthly entity needs to be flawless in order to be hailed as respectable, then no such entity exists!

Younger generations are particularly vulnerable to the aforementioned media influences. After years of indoctrination in educational and entertainment systems saturated with a secular humanistic viewpoint, it's no wonder that as adults many of those voters send those with a similar approach into governments at every level. At that point those anti-biblical ideas become not just personal philosophy, but generally accepted public policy. In some cases they become actual law! Many morally responsible laws are eliminated, and new ones are passed which demand complicity with, or even endorsement of, immorality. The Bible that has been the historical foundation of our legal system through Blackstone's *Commentaries on the Laws*, has been thrown aside and ridiculed by many in leadership.

When the power of the prevailing culture ascends to the institution of government, it's reached it's apex. While education and media can influence intellectually and emotionally, government can broadly control behavior through the instrument of punishment. It can reduce your finances through fines or restrict your freedom by confining you behind bars. No wonder Proverbs 28:12 informs us that: "When the righteous triumph, there is great elation; but when the wicked rise to power, men go into hiding." Leaders without divine moorings are the bane of any society, and are even prone to become dictatorial.

Governmental institutions at every level have often led us away from the biblical standards which had historically been the basis of their authority. From the president, congress, and supreme and federal appeals courts... to governors, state legislatures, and state courts... to county and municipal governmental bodies and officials... even down to local school boards... they are each through their laws, rulings, orders, and policies placing increasing restrictions upon churches and Christian individuals' ability to exercise their beliefs. They're demoralizingly pecking away at our first amendment rights.

We're at a tipping point when it comes to a largely godless and lawless popular national culture potentially taking full control of our governments. It's a moral and political disaster just waiting to happen.

In Deuteronomy 29:23-25 God warned the nation of Israel of severe judgment if they abandoned their legacy in Him. "It will be like the destruction of Sodom and Gomorrah, Admah and Zeboiim, which the LORD overthrew in fierce anger. All the nations will ask: 'Why has the LORD done this to this land? Why this fierce, burning anger?' And the answer will be: 'It is because this people abandoned the covenant of the LORD, the God of their fathers...'" This forewarning came to fruition as centuries later both of Israel's divided kingdoms turned away from their heritage in the Lord.

First the northern kingdom of Israel fell to the Assyrian empire because "They rejected his (Yahweh's) decrees and the covenant he had made with their fathers and the warnings he had given them. They followed worthless idols and themselves became worthless. They imitated the nations around them although the LORD had ordered them, 'Do not do as they do,' and they did the things the LORD had forbidden them to do" (II Kings 17:15). Their leaders had led them into sin.

The destruction of the southern kingdom of Judah, whose spiritual decline had taken longer, followed later. But the cause was the same. They had forsaken the God of Abraham and become like the surrounding pagan idolaters. "...They did more evil than the nations the LORD had destroyed before the Israelites" (II Kings 21:9). This was the aftermath of the wicked reign of the most ungodly king in their history.

Leadership is a critical element in the fate of nations. In America we have the incredible right and responsibility to choose our leaders. Voters need to recognize the critical choices in front of us... especially Bible-believing Christian voters! American citizens have been given this privilege of picking our governmental leaders. Will we choose politically correct leaders or biblically correct leaders? The future hangs in the balance and the decision is ours as a nation!

The very first Chief Justice of the U.S. Supreme Court had something to say on that issue. Justice John Jay advised: "Providence has given to our people the choice of their rulers, and it is the duty, as well as the privilege and interest, of our Christian nation to select and prefer Christians for their rulers."

The United States has suffered discipline from the Lord for our earlier wanderings from godly standards, and in the more recent past we have begun again to come under divine chastisement for our backsliding. Such discipline is designed by God to bring us back into the faith and obedience which has allowed Him to bless and use us as few other countries in history. In spite of this, we have continued in the last few decades to move farther away from His will. If we refuse to repent, His chastisements will intensify, and ultimately move into the realm of divine judgment. This happened to the nation of Israel, and we are no exception to this pattern of the Lord's dealings with His people.

As Israel did on more than one occasion, so we have in recent times very much surrendered to the allure of the values of a corrupt society. That worldly culture has turned true righteous standards upside down. God's prophet Isaiah was directed by Him to give a dire warning to the Jews when they had yielded to the idolatry of those around them. "Woe to those who call evil good and good evil, who put darkness for light and light for darkness, who put bitter for sweet and sweet for bitter" (Isaiah 5:20).

A *political shift* in our nation may provide temporary relief from the failures of a socialistic, secular humanistic governing philosophy, but only a real *spiritual awakening* is a long-term escape from such a dilemma. Our current problems have deeper roots than just a political *mindset*. The country's *heart* has been turned away from the Lord and His Word. Only a widespread heart and soul return to Him will restore the Christian values we've tragically lost.

So, will America increasingly yield to the misdirected cultural influence which permeates much of society and become more and more like Sodom and Gomorrah until the mercy of God must give way to the judgment of God? Will people of faith in this country be like Lot, so caught up in the surrounding moral climate that we have no effective ability to provoke a righteous change of direction? Or will we like Abraham stand firm on our covenant with the Lord, and be a godly influence upon those around us, interceding for and rescuing the lost whenever possible?

In a quote often attributed to 18th century God-fearing British statesman Edmund Burke, there is foreboding caution. President John F. Kennedy actually referred to this statement in a 1961 speech to the Canadian Parliament, crediting Burke. Though the actual origin of it cannot be confirmed, history has nonetheless evidenced its veracity. Americans would do well to heed its warning. "All that is necessary for the triumph of evil is that good men do nothing." We must to stand up against the evil threatening our God-ordained freedoms or we will lose them!

If America is ever to return to our sacred footings, the Body of Christ must take the lead. Many of us have become too much conformed to the world around us. This nation has been prone to wander from the ways of the Lord. We need to get back on the narrow path (see Matthew 7:13). The godly influence of the church upon this society must surpass that of its dominant godless culture. How might we accomplish that? We'll address that question in the final chapter.

Chapter 6

The Ancient Paradigm Recurs, Part 2

(The American Church)

Of even greater concern than the decline of the American nation is the decline of the American church. At the outset let me state that I know that I'll be speaking in generalities here. Individuals, congregations and church groups (including in a less homogeneous sense, various denominations) have taken different courses in recent times. Plus, the degrees to which such individuals and groups have maintained, or turned away from, sound Scriptural standards varies. But our spiritual wanderings are undeniable.

In previous generations the church was the major influence on American culture. Despite our imperfections we were predominately a force for the good of society. In this current generation the tendency has been just the opposite. Popular culture has been the major influence on the church... and mostly *not* with beneficial effect. Some aspects of our contemporary national culture can be positive. Some features are neutral. Still, far too much of it stands in opposition to the Creator's good and holy designs for mankind, and the bulk of its effect on the church has been harmful, leading Christian groups away from biblical truths. This is what happened to Lot as he gradually fell under the influence of the culture of the twin wicked cities of Sodom and Gomorrah.

The church in America, as with the children of God in Israel, would have done well to follow the Lord's commands to refuse to allow the wickedness of the heathen to corrupt us. Psalm 106:34-37 reports that after entering the Promised Land: "They did not destroy the peoples as the LORD had commanded them, but they mingled with the nations and adopted their customs. They worshiped their idols, which became a snare to them. They sacrificed their sons and daughters to demons." When I consider the latter sentence in that passage I can't help but equate that ancient evil with the modern slaughter of millions of innocent children *in* (and now *even out of*) their mothers' wombs.

The problem in much of the American church is not simply that we're surrounded by a sinful culture, it's that we're allowing that culture's standards to seep into our individual lives, families, and churches. Someone once put it this way: "Ships don't sink because of the water <u>around</u> them. Ships sink because of the water that <u>gets into</u> them." In His high priestly prayer for His followers recorded in John chapter 17, Jesus made a similar distinction. In verse 11 He proclaimed to His Father that we *"are still in* the world," but then in verse 14 He reminded the Father that we *are not of* the world."

The principle of avoiding the polluting influence of those in rebellion against God is clearly carried over into the New Testament as well. In Romans 12:2 we're commanded "Do not conform any longer to the pattern of this world, but be transformed by the renewing of your mind. Then you will be able to test and approve what God's will is—his good, pleasing and perfect will." I Corinthians 15:33 warns: "Bad company corrupts good character." II Corinthians 6:14 advises: "Do not be yoked together with unbelievers." It then goes on to ask the questions: "For what do righteousness and wickedness have in common? Or what fellowship can light have with darkness?"

This is not to say that we should despise and mistreat sinners. What it means is that we should never be yoked with non-Christians in the sense of jointly serving the flesh and the devil. Our contrasting lifestyle must be a glowing example of what God wants all men and women to be. Jesus is the light of the world (see John 12:46), and as His followers we are to reflect His light into the lives of those who are lost in the darkness of sin (see Matthew 5:14). God loves every sinner (including *us*) and so should we. Christians who allow their hatred of wickedness to become hatred of wicked people have turned the Gospel on its head. "But God demonstrates his own love for us in this: While we were still sinners, Christ died for us" (Romans 5:8).

When confronted with the woman caught in the act of adultery, Jesus treated her with love, offering her forgiveness, but told her to "Go now and *leave your life of sin*" (John 8:11). We should love sinners. Yet we must hate sin (theirs *or ours*), and never excuse or endorse it. Love of sinners and hatred of sin are not incompatible. Romans 12:9 Paul says: "Love must be sincere. Hate what is evil; cling to what is good." In Psalm 101:3 David says: "The deeds of faithless men I hate; they will not cling to me."

I vividly remember my experience at "Stand in the Gap: A Sacred Assembly of Men," a Promise Keepers event on the National Mall in Washington D. C. on October 4, 1997. We were gathering as Christian men to repent of our sins and pray for America. I had traveled with hundreds of other men to the event from the Hudson Valley of New York state on a train chartered for that purpose. For some reason the train was late in arriving at our destination.

Leaving the train station to hurry to the gathering, we walked quickly so as to miss as little of the activities as possible. Various groups lined the way... some supportive of our mission of prayer for the nation... some vehemently opposing it. I remember one particularly hateful crowd held signs which read: "CHRISTIANS, NO! LIONS, YES!" Among our opponents was a small gathering of gay activists. As we passed by they chanted: "Two, four, six, eight, end this homophobic hate!"

I wanted to stop and address them, but I didn't know my way around D.C., and feared I would become separated from my fellow train passengers and get lost. To this day I wonder if I should have simply trusted the Lord to guide me, stood still, and told them the truth about how real Christians felt. "Who told you we hate you? We don't hate you. We love you. So does Jesus! We do hate your sin. It can doom you to hell, and we want you to go to Heaven." It's vital that we recall that *repentance* is an indispensable part of salvation.

There is an inclination among many in contemporary Christianity to rarely if ever speak against sin, lest we offend the sinner. We seem to believe that shame for misbehavior is a terrible thing. Scripture, however, teaches that godly shame is a good and necessary emotion. In Jeremiah 6:15 the Lord laments the lack of such shame. "'Are they ashamed of their loathsome conduct? No, they have no shame at all; they do not even know how to blush. So they will fall among the fallen; they will be brought down when I punish them,' says the LORD."

Shame is an essential precursor to repentance and forgiveness. God is not endorsing a lifestyle of constant shame and condemnation, but moments of shame for sin that lead to salvation for sinners, and restoration of sweet fellowship for saints. I John 1:8,9 says: "If we claim to be without sin, we deceive ourselves and the truth is not in us. If we confess our sins, he is faithful and just and will forgive us our sins and purify us from all unrighteousness."

Jesus' love for the lost never made him hesitate to speak out against ungodliness. He knew what His Father had said about our responsibility to warn sinners of judgment. "When I say to a wicked man, 'You will surely die,' and you do not warn him or speak out to dissuade him from his evil ways in order to save his life, that wicked man will die for his sin, and I will hold you accountable for his blood" (Ezekiel 3:18).

John the Baptist, the forerunner of Jesus, preached repentance so that people might receive the precious gift of forgiveness from God. A loving Christ looked upon the crowds gathered before Him with deep compassion, longing for them to come to God. Yet both of them referred to these sinners as a "brood of vipers" (see Luke 3:7 and

Matthew 23:33). In Luke 13:32 Jesus even referred to Herod Antipas as "that fox." Scholars report that this use of "fox" meant a person of cunning and treachery... that a modern day equivalent might be calling someone a "rat"

The Master instructed His disciples to also speak out boldly and publicly to warn against the dire consequences of sin. "When you enter a town and are welcomed, eat what is set before you. Heal the sick who are there and tell them, 'The kingdom of God is near you.' But when you enter a town and are not welcomed, go into its streets and say, *'Even the dust of your town that sticks to our feet we wipe off against you.* Yet be sure of this: The kingdom of God is near.' I tell you, it will be more bearable on that day for Sodom than for that town" (Luke 10:8-12). In this current moral and political climate, can you imagine the angry reaction if we were to obey that command of Jesus today?

There are numerous instances in the gospels which make it clear that Christ was not afraid of offending sinners by calling out their sin. They needed to know they were sinners before they could repent and receive Him as their Savior.

And what about offending a holy and loving Creator? When unbelievers rail against His sovereignty and His rules for righteous living, should we be silent? Here's what notable Reformation theologian John Calvin had to say: "A dog barks when his master is attacked. I would be a coward if I saw that God's truth is attacked and yet would remain silent." Compassion for lost sinners does not demand that we bite our tongues when the Lord and His Word are ridiculed. In Ephesians 4:15 we're instructed to be "...speaking the truth in love."

Preacher and author Leonard Ravenhill noted what he believed was the reason for the more enduring results of one renowned evangelist's ministry over another. "Finney never made an altar call within the first twenty eight nights of preaching. Most of our evangelists don't have twenty eight sermons. Twenty eight nights in a row and he never made an altar call. He didn't preach the love of God. He didn't say 'you're a sinner, God loves you.' He said 'God is angry with the wicked every day' (Psalm 7:11) which the Word of God says... He didn't preach love, he preached judgment... He didn't say 'you're a wonderful person' he said 'you're a rebel.' But he got results. 64% of D. L. Moody's converts *backslid*, 72% of the converts Finney got, *stood*, because he knew how to attack the human will, not just the emotions."

The above comparison is a rather disproportionate example. Nevertheless it points out the importance of preaching about divine judgment as well as divine love. Balance is a key factor in properly dealing with the Word of God. We may like to only peruse and preach the attributes of God which we or others personally prefer, but we must honor the full scope of the Bible's presentation of the nature of God. Either we believe *all* of Scripture is divinely inspired, or we don't.

Romans 11:22 urges an honest and balanced approach to viewing God's character. "Consider therefore the *kindness* and *sternness* of God: *sternness* to those who fell, but *kindness* to you, provided that you continue in his kindness. Otherwise, you also will be cut off." This verse show us that neither of these two divine attributes negates the other, that recognizing both these aspects are necessary if we want to understand the God we serve.

Want to be wise in the things of God? "The fear of the LORD is the beginning of knowledge, but fools despise wisdom and discipline" (Proverbs 1:7).

Preacher and author A. W. Tozer explained the reconciliation of these two features of God's nature this way: "God is never at cross-purposes with Himself. No attribute of God is in conflict with another. God's compassion flows out of his goodness, and goodness without justice is not goodness. God spares us because He is good, but He could not be good if He were not just." Theologian G. K. Chesterson put it his way: "[Christianity is] not an amalgam(ation) or compromise, but both things at the top of their energy; love and wrath both burning. Christianity is a superhuman paradox whereby two opposite passions may blaze beside each other."

The Lord provides a guard against the dire consequences of being "cut off" cited in the latter part of Romans 11:22. It's called discipline. Hebrews 12:5-9 explains this beneficial process. "'My son, do not make light of the Lord's discipline, and do not lose heart when he rebukes you, because the Lord disciplines those he loves, and he punishes everyone he accepts as a son.' Endure hardship as discipline; God is treating you as sons. For what son is not disciplined by his father? If you are not disciplined (and everyone undergoes discipline), then you are illegitimate children and not true sons. Moreover, we have all had human fathers who disciplined us and we respected them for it. How much more should we submit to the Father of our spirits and live!"

Unrepentant sinners will receive *judgment*. Faithful believers receive *discipline*. Judgment is the final consequence of wickedness. Discipline is the ongoing safeguard against falling back into unbelief, disobedience, and judgment. The purpose of judgment is to condemn those who refuse to repent and submit to God. The purpose of discipline is to shape Christians into the image of Jesus and help us maintain our relationship to God as His children. Let's preach the *whole* Gospel in order to bring rebels into the family of God where they come under the loving discipline of a loving Heavenly Father, rather than the eternal judgment of a Holy God.

Many want to restrict the judgment of God to the Old Testament alone. I remind you of what I pointed out in the introduction of this book. According to Scripture the essential nature of the Lord does not change. In Malachi 3:6 He Himself proclaims "I the LORD do not change." In Hebrews 13:8 the inspired writer attributes that same standard to the Son of God. "Jesus Christ is the same yesterday and today and forever." Divine judgment occurs not only under the *old* covenant, but the *new* covenant as well… and not just at the end of time as noted in the book of Revelation. The book of Acts demonstrates instances of, and warnings about, judgment during the history of the first century church.

Acts 5:1-11 records the account of Ananias and Sapphira being struck dead for lying to the Holy Spirit. Acts 8:18-24 tells how a man named Simon bargained to buy the supernatural ability to bestow the Holy Spirit on whomever he chose. Peter warned him to repent of such a sinful attitude lest he too be struck dead. And Acts 12:19-23 chronicles the death of a ruler who in pride welcomed a fawning crowd's assignment of divinity to him personally. Herod was consequently struck down, eaten by worms, and died on the spot!

Our job is not to accept the standards of the world, and certainly not to conform to them! I love the word the old King James Version uses to describe our uniqueness in I Peter 2:9,10. "But ye are a chosen generation, a royal priesthood, an holy nation, a **peculiar** people; that ye should shew forth the praises of him who hath called you out of darkness into his marvellous light: Which in time past were not a people, but are now the people of God: which had not obtained mercy, but now have obtained mercy."

Let's not be afraid to be different from those around us when it comes to moral standards. We must love them, but not affirm their lifestyles… and certainly not become like them! Jude verse 4 warns of deceitful people who rub shoulders with true Christians in an effort to promote a devilish distortion of God's grace. "For certain men whose condemnation was written about long ago have secretly slipped in among you. They are godless men, who change the grace of our God into a license for immorality and deny Jesus Christ our only Sovereign and Lord."

And in our efforts to reach the lost, let's not forget that rebellion stirs God's anger and wrath. The Bible nowhere suggests that the Lord never gets angry at men and women who deliberately disobey His commands. It does repeatedly tell us that *He is slow to anger*, and that *His anger lasts only for a moment* (Psalm 30:5). I John chapter 4 twice declares that wonderful three word truth: "God is love." Still, it doesn't suggest that love never gets angry. I Corinthians 13:5 maintains that love "...*is not easily angered.*" Divine anger is restrained to some degree by divine love. But both unbelievers and believers still can incite the Lord's anger by rebelling against His sovereign will.

Over the years I've witnessed an increasing tendency on the part of many in Christian ministry to re-interpret certain Scriptures based upon culture. This inclination is dangerous and often results in outright error. It begins by assigning the truths, commands, and instructions of certain passages strictly to the culture of the historical era in which that passage was written. Those particular verses are then dismissed as no longer relevant or in force today. As a further result, God's Word on those issues must then be brought into alignment with today's prevailing culture. An example of the results of this approach is how some have declared that homosexuality must no longer be considered sin because it was only said in the Bible to be sin because that was the narrow view in the culture during which Scripture was written.

This approach to biblical interpretation contradicts what Scripture says about itself. "All Scripture is God-breathed and is useful for teaching, rebuking, correcting and training in righteousness, so that the man of God may be thoroughly equipped for every good work" (II Timothy 3:16,17). It does not state that *most* Scripture, or *some* Scripture is divinely inspired... It clearly asserts that *all* Scripture is God-breathed... not born of contemporaneous culture. Either we believe that or we don't. There is no middle ground.

II Peter 1:20,21 affirms this same fact. "Above all, you must understand that no prophecy of Scripture came about by the prophet's own interpretation. For prophecy never had its origin in the will of man, but men spoke from God as they were carried along by the Holy Spirit."

And II Peter 3:15,16 applies this standard not only to the Old Testament books, but to the New Testament books as well. "Bear in mind that our Lord's patience means salvation, just as our dear brother Paul also wrote you with the wisdom that God gave him. He writes the same way in all his letters, speaking in them of these matters. His letters contain some things that are hard to understand, which ignorant and unstable people distort, as they do the other Scriptures, to their own destruction."

Of course there are statements in the Bible which are quoted as the words of human beings, and do not necessarily represent truth from the Lord Himself. For instance, Psalm 14:1 and Psalm 53:1 both state: "There is no God." However, the context tells us that these four words are not divine truth, but the statement of a *fool*. Then there are passages like I Corinthians chapter 7, where Paul goes back and forth between clear commands from the Lord, and his own personal advice, relating to marriage. Romans chapter 14 also expounds on areas of Christian living that can legitimately vary from one individual believer to another. We commonly refer to such standards as "personal convictions." We must study Scripture carefully and prayerfully to sort out these various kinds of distinctions.

Uncovering the cultural background of sections of God's Word can provide historical context and help us more fully grasp the truths found in those passages, but we must not attribute the origin of divine commands to human customs. Some features of contemporary culture can also be used as tools to help reach the lost. That's what the Apostle Paul did in Athens, Greece. Acts 17:16-34 tells how he used a pagan altar labeled "To an Unknown

God" as a springboard to present the facts about the true God. He did not, however, go on to endorse their idolatry or accept their false gods.

We must be careful. Once we begin to disregard some Bible portions based upon the theory that they've originated only because of the influence of ancient society, we can deny divine inspiration. Then we may pick and choose which ones fit with modern mores and which ones don't... or even which ones we personally like and which ones we don't! The Word of God thus becomes the word of men.

Grant it, there are parts of the Bible that are hard to understand, and parts that are not very palatable to the human mind or emotions. I've been reading and studying Scripture for some six decades and there are portions of it I still don't fully comprehend... even things in it which make me uncomfortable. Yet there is much I've learned and come to better understand over the course of time. And when I enter the eternal fullness of God's Presence, my knowledge of Him and His Word will no longer suffer from the limitations imposed by this present existence.

I think of what the Apostle Paul said in I Corinthians 13:9-12. "For we know in part and we prophesy in part, but when perfection comes, the imperfect disappears. When I was a child, I talked like a child, I thought like a child, I reasoned like a child. When I became a man, I put childish ways behind me. Now we see but a poor reflection as in a mirror; then we shall see face to face. Now I know in part; then I shall know fully, even as I am fully known." Until that moment arrives I'll continue to believe in the verbal inspiration of all Scripture. Faith and the undeniable proof of design in nature have taught me the validity of belief in the Creator. In addition, numerous supernatural events in my life which are consistent with the Bible have helped to confirm my confidence in its divine origin.

Many years ago the Lord taught me how vital *balance* is when it comes to studying and teaching the Word. As fallen human beings we're by nature inclined toward extremes. Even as Christians we tend to vacillate from one form of immoderation to another: from legalism to licentiousness, from vows of poverty to claims on material prosperity, from cold liturgy to cozy disrespect. Thus we often want to emphasize one aspect of Bible truth, while ignoring or denying another which may be the flip side of the first. The outcome is that our spiritual vision becomes distorted and we eventually no longer recognize the full scope of Scripture's verity.

Let me offer a parallel from the natural realm. If we only ever see pennies with the head of Lincoln facing up, and then we ultimately see one with the Lincoln Memorial revealed instead, we'll be prone to say "that's not a real penny!" The same kind of thing can happen in the spiritual world. God help us to live and walk in the balance of His sacred truths!

Many in Christian ministry have simply lost such biblical balance, resulting in a lack of spiritual equilibrium for themselves and those whom they serve. But it sometimes gets worse. Tying the meaning of Scripture to human culture is the entrance to a road that can ultimately lead to heresy and apostasy.

It's common for those of us in leadership in the Body of Christ to have a particular emphasis in our ministry. Some of this may stem from our natural temperaments. These are considered the gifts we are born with. They're

SAM MASON

listed in Romans 12:6-8, and are referred to by many as the "motivational gifts." I also believe that our ministry emphases are likely part of our calling from God.

These individual ministry focuses can be blessings from the Lord to His people. But we must guard against allowing them to morph into scripturally unbalanced error. Personal preferences must not become their motivation. We must also be careful not to let our ministry emphasis artificially narrow our approach to preaching Bible truth. We may begin to totally neglect other divine teachings that are also essential to walking with God. Worse yet, we may come to the place where we outright deny certain commands and doctrines that we have decided are now unpalatable.

With grave concern in recent years I've witnessed quite a number of well known preachers and teachers begin to contradict Bible principles and commands on some very basic issues. They've yielded to the assertions of the prevailing western culture and its political correctness on matters of sexuality and gender identity. Sexual relations were created by God for procreation, physical intimacy, and mutual pleasure. But they were only intended to be practiced between one husband (male) and one wife (female).

Of particular concern in these areas of sex and gender is the about face on homosexuality and transgenderism made by some of these ministers. Both Old and New Testament passages clearly identify homosexuality as perversion of God's creative design, yet these so-called Bible teachers are declaring that it is not sin! They buy into the unscientific proposal that some men and women are born to be homosexual or transgender.

The Almighty designed *all* mankind in His own likeness, but Genesis 1:27 also definitively certifies that He established 2 (*not* as some have asserted: 3, 63, or even 112) distinct sexual types of human beings. "So God created man in his own image, in the image of God he created him; male and female he created them." The Lord not only created them unique physically, but different in other ways as well. While both genders are equally loved and valued in His eyes, and share certain common traits, we're meant to maintain the diversities of divine design. The Bible even offers various means of demonstrating and maintaining the separate identities of men and women, including aspects of appearance and roles.

These gender distinctions need to be maintained in the Body of Christ too. Although the accounts in Scripture show that God more often calls men to positions of ministry and leadership, He clearly uses women in those areas as well. We see many examples of that in both Old and New Testaments. That doesn't mean, however, that women must become more like men in order to lead. I came across an interesting statement I first saw on a particular woman's Facebook page. To me, it put it quite well. In my effort to determine its origin, I found that same statement quoted on several internet sites. I was unable to ascertain where or from whom it originated, but it communicated the truth so succinctly that I wanted to share it anyway.

"Our generation is becoming so busy trying to prove that women can do what men can do, that women are losing their uniqueness. Women weren't created to do everything a man *can* do. Women were created to do everything a man *can't* do."

Having established the transcendent authority of

Scripture over all facets of our lives, it's vital that we learn and absorb its truths. We should regularly sit under the sound preaching and teaching of the Word in fellowship with others of like precious faith, and read other solidly Bible-based books which can help us grow in our knowledge of it. The most essential exercise for every child of God, however, is to personally read and study the Bible daily, then by the Lord's grace to increasingly walk in His will as expressed in *the Book*.

Exercising restrictions on ministering the whole counsel of God will have ill effects on our evangelistic endeavors. Sinners need to know that God is both Savior and Judge… that sin is still sin as long as the Bible says so, no matter what society declares. That the Creator loves sinners with an incredible love, and wants to both *forgive them* and *deliver them* from their destructive sinful lifestyles.

Limiting how much divine truth we talk about also has a detrimental impact on believers' growth in grace and the knowledge of of our Lord (see II Peter 3:18). Matthew 28:18-20, referred to as "The Great Commission," commands us not just to preach the Gospel, but to "…make disciples" (literally disciplined ones), "…teaching them to obey everything I have commanded you." Remember, discipline is to be the lot of every true child of God. The Lord disciplines us because He loves us. Divine discipline is not particularly fun, but it's for our good. "No discipline seems pleasant at the time, but painful. Later on, however, it produces a harvest of righteousness and peace for those who have been trained by it" (Hebrews 12:11).

As followers of Christ, our thoughts, words, and deeds should line up as much as possible with His example and teachings. We're not yet perfect, but our godly witness should be strong enough to reflect His light into the darkness of this world. We may be the only Jesus some may ever see. For that light to shine *fully*, we need to *fully* embrace the whole Word of God.

The Scriptural imbalance relating to divine mercy and judgment is probably the most widespread digression, but there are others. It's our compromise of God's Word that is the starting point of our decline. Having bought into popular culture to one degree or another, we've ceased teaching and practicing the *whole counsel* of the Lord.

Another area where we need to return to balance is in what the Word of God has to say about riches and poverty. Just as Lot had lost his spiritual moorings in the areas of separation from worldly ways, and the balance between divine mercy and judgment, his perspective on the issue of material blessings had become distorted. This overwrought desire for earthly prosperity appears to have been the initial motivation for his separation from the godly influence of his uncle Abraham, and his eventual drift into the ungodly influence of the culture of Sodom and Gomorrah.

"Lot looked up and saw that the whole plain of the Jordan was well watered, like the garden of the LORD, like the land of Egypt, toward Zoar. (This was before the LORD destroyed Sodom and Gomorrah.) So Lot chose for himself the whole plain of the Jordan and set out toward the east. The two men parted company: Abram lived in the land of Canaan, while Lot lived among the cities of the plain and pitched his tents near Sodom" (Genesis 13:10-12).

This is not to say that riches are in and of themselves

sinful. Abraham and many other heroes of the faith were wealthy. The Bible places no spiritual premium on riches or poverty. The heart of the issue is the attitude of the heart. Paul taught the believers in Philippi that contentment was the key. "...For I have learned to be content whatever the circumstances. I know what it is to be in need, and I know what it is to have plenty. I have learned the secret of being content in any and every situation, whether well fed or hungry, whether living in plenty or in want. I can do everything through him who gives me strength" (Philippians 4:11-13).

In His parable of the sower, Jesus warned of the potential negative impact of riches upon the positive effect of the Word of God. "...But the worries of this life, the deceitfulness of wealth and the desires for other things come in and choke the word" (Mark 4:19). Our primary focus in life should be upon things of eternal value. Christ pointed His disciples in this direction. "Do not store up for yourselves treasures on earth, where moth and rust destroy, and where thieves break in and steal. But store up for yourselves treasures in heaven, where moth and rust do not destroy, and where thieves do not break in and steal. For where your treasure is, there your heart will be also" (Matthew 6:19-21).

Lot became focused on material prosperity and suffered great loss. Abraham concentrated on his relationship with the Lord and received lavish spiritual blessings that would be extended not only to his own descendants, but to "all peoples on earth." Abraham's vision in life was an eternal one. I remind you of the Bible passage we quoted in chapter 3 of this book. "By faith he made his home in the promised land like a stranger in a foreign country; he lived in tents, as did Isaac and Jacob, who were heirs with him of the same promise. For he was looking forward to the city with foundations, whose architect and builder is God" (Hebrews 11:9,10).

Will we as the Body of Christ follow the example of Lot, or the pattern of Abraham? Will we live to keep up with the Joneses, or to follow in the footsteps of Jesus. Will we conform to the greedy culture of the world, or be a godly witness of life's divine best to the lost world for whom Jesus died?

It's easy to be caught up in the lusts of the flesh, it's a challenge to seek to please God in all things. While Abraham is a fine spiritual model, the example set by Jesus is the supreme one. He never strayed from the will of His Father. "...I do nothing on my own but speak just what the Father has taught me. The one who sent me is with me; he has not left me alone, for I always do what pleases him" (John 8:28,29). Like Abraham we are imperfect, but we must never be content with that as a static condition and settle down in it. As II Corinthians 13:11 urges us, we should "Aim for perfection." We should never stop growing in the Lord.

The Apostle Paul described his ongoing spiritual journey as a *lifelong* pursuit. "But whatever was to my profit I now consider loss for the sake of Christ. What is more, I consider everything a loss compared to the surpassing greatness of knowing Christ Jesus my Lord, for whose sake I have lost all things. I consider them rubbish, that I may gain Christ and be found in him, not having a righteousness of my own that comes from the law, but that which is through faith in Christ—the righteousness that comes from God and is by faith. I want to know Christ and the power of his resurrection and the fellowship of sharing in his sufferings, becoming like him in his death, and so, somehow, to attain to the resurrection from the dead. Not that I have already obtained all this, or have already been made perfect, but I press on to take hold of that for which Christ Jesus took hold of me. Brothers, I do not consider myself yet to have taken hold of it. But one thing I do: Forgetting what is behind and straining toward what is ahead, I press on toward the goal to win the prize for which God has called me heavenward in Christ Jesus. All of us who are mature should take such a view of things. And if on some point you think differently, that too God will make clear to you. Only let us live up to what we have already attained" (Philippians 3:7-16).

There are other Bible truths from which we've strayed, or at the least lost our balance on, but we won't take the time here to detail them all. It is vital though, that if we have wandered from the truth of God, we come back home to it. Jude was deeply concerned with such dangerous spiritual digressions. In verse 7 of his book, Jude offers the twin wicked cities of Lot's day as an illustration of the tragic fate which ultimately awaits those who stray from faith in God's Word into the error of the devil and then unbelief. "In a similar way, Sodom and Gomorrah and the surrounding towns gave themselves up to sexual immorality and perversion. They serve as an example of those who suffer the punishment of eternal fire."

If we've compromised the Scriptures by attempting to conform them to the political correctness of the current popular culture, we desperately need to return to them as the verbally and divinely inspired Word of the living God. Only by doing so can we right ourselves with the

Lord... and only then can we have the kind of righteous impact on America that our forefathers did. It's a matter of repentance, forgiveness, and restoration.

If we've simply gotten a little off course, we can more readily move back to the center of the road. If our wanderings have carried us far astray we must claim the promise of God to us in II Chronicles 7:14. "...If my people, who are called by my name, will humble themselves and pray and seek my face and turn from their wicked ways, then will I hear from heaven and will forgive their sin and will heal their land." Yes, our prayer is that our nation itself come to repentance and faith, but it has to begin with us as God's people. "For it is time for judgment to begin with the family of God; and if it begins with us, what will the outcome be for those who do not obey the gospel of God?" (I Peter 4:17).

If necessary, our attempt to make a real difference in America must start with our own repentance as Christians. Where does it go from there? What actions on our part can help bring our beloved nation back to its blessed roots in the God of our fathers?

All that is good and right in life springs from the heart of the Maker of the Universe. The highway through which it all travels is our active relationship with Him. The Greek word commonly used in the New Testament for this divine fellowship is: "koinonia." In his *Expository Dictionary of New Testament Words*, W. E. Vine gives its definition as "communion, fellowship, sharing in common." If we want to enjoy its benefits and demonstrate them to others, we need to regularly exercise this blessed kinship with the Almighty.

The two great pillars of this "koinonia" are prayer and

the Word. Put simply: prayer is us talking to God, the Word is God talking to us. Fellowship with our Heavenly Father is a two-way street. Keeping it moving in both directions is essential to living the Christian life. It's also essential to enabling us to be the light of the gospel shining in the darkness of this fallen world... empowering us to make a godly difference in the lives of those around us.

Let's first talk a little more about the Word of God. The Bible is the *written* Word of God. Here in America, as in much of the world, we have the blessing of Scripture in print readily available to us. That's a gift we should never take for granted. Many others across the globe have no such easy access to the most valuable book on earth. Yet how many of us leave it on a bookshelf, coffee table, or nightstand gathering dust?

I recall many years ago hearing the eye-opening testimony of an older man in our church. He had been diagnosed with prostate cancer some months earlier. He stood to his feet during the service and told how he had been a Christian and regularly attended church nearly his whole life, yet had never made a habit of reading his Bible! He went on to tell what a blessing he was now enjoying since he'd begun daily reading and studying the Word of God.

Sitting under sound Bible preaching and teaching is a vital part of our walk with the Lord, but it cannot take the place of personally searching the Scripture. You say you find it difficult to understand some passages? So do I! I've been reading and studying the Word of God since childhood, and there are still portions I don't fully grasp. I have, however, learned so much over a lifetime, and continue to grow spiritually as I daily open the Book. Don't think that because you don't have a degree in theology you can't excavate the spiritual riches our Heavenly Father deposited in the Bible.

Scripture is the foundation of God's Word for believers, but it's not the only channel through which God speaks to His children. He talks to us in various ways. He communicates by way of the aforementioned preaching and teaching of those truly called and gifted to do so. His voice can sometimes be heard through fellow believers as they share divine inspiration born of their experience, or are prompted by some of the gifts of the Holy Spirit to share a word from the Lord with us. On occasions God communicates to us through our circumstances. If we're sensitive enough we can also hear His "still small voice" inside our hearts, or on rare occasions perhaps even an audible voice. To some God may speak through dreams and visions.

While we should be open to the various means through which the Lord may communicate with us, we also need to be circumspect. Scripture cautions us to "test the spirits to see whether they are from God..." (I John 4:1). Whatever other channel He uses to talk to us, God will never contradict His written Word, the Bible.

Now let's briefly discuss prayer. Prayer is a subject too deep and wide for a full treatment in a few paragraphs. But I do want to share some essentials.

Foremost among those essentials is the fact that prayer only works if we have faith in God. Jesus taught us that "If you believe, you will receive whatever you ask for in prayer" (Matthew 21:22). Faith cannot be generated by our human minds. It is a divine impartation. Positive thinking is fine, but faith does not come from that. It's given to us by our Heavenly Father.

In Romans 12:3 Paul encourages humility, pointing out that our faith comes from the Lord. "...Think of yourself with sober judgment, in accordance with the measure of faith God has given you." What is the conduit of this divine gift? "...Faith comes from hearing the message, and the message is heard through the word of Christ" (Romans 10:17). It's the truth of God's Word that produces faith. Faith knows that the Almighty is the Truth, and Satan and anyone or anything else that contradicts His Word is a liar. Faith comes only from the Lord Himself. We can increase our faith by exercising it, but we cannot in and of ourselves create it.

Prayer is commonly perceived through a narrow lens. We tend to think of it primarily, if not exclusively, as asking God for things. It is that, but it's much broader than that. It includes everything our heart utters to the Lord. Let me just touch on six expressions of prayer mentioned in Scripture.

(1) *Petition or supplication* is requesting things from God. This is the sole purpose of prayer as most folks would define it. Prayer is not limited to asking for things, but it certainly is an important part of it. A higher form of supplication and petition is (2) *intercession*. The Greek word "huperentunchano," meaning "to make a petition or intercede on behalf of another," is used only once in the entire New Testament. In Romans 8:26 it speaks of the Holy Spirit praying through us. It's truly a supernatural function. Our praying in tongues is one way the Spirit does this. (3) *Confession* can be both negative and positive. We can and should confess our sins and weaknesses to

the Lord. It may also be simply pouring out our feelings to God about what is happening to us, or around us. These three expressions of prayer tend to be human-oriented. The next three are God-oriented.

(4) *Thanksgiving* is our response to to the acts of God which directly benefit us. It will help us focus on God's goodness to us. (5) *Praise* focuses on the works of the Lord in a more general sense: His might, His power, the wonders of His creation, etc. (6) *Worship* is the highest expression of prayer. It centers on Who He is. It's our reaction to His glorious person, and can only be done in the spirit. Jesus declared "Yet a time is coming and has now come when the true worshipers will worship the Father in spirit and truth, for they are the kind of worshipers the Father seeks. God is spirit, and his worshipers must worship in spirit and in truth" (John 4:23,24).

As we draw closer to the Lord through our sacred conversational relationship with Him, life will become more of the joy it was meant to be from the beginning. Prayer and the Word flow back and forth between Father and child, and our lives are enriched. Then that life can be more effectively shared with those around us. We pray for others to know Him and we live and speak of the Word of God that offers real life to all mankind. Our witness for Christ becomes empowered by the Holy Spirit Who lives in and through us.

Of course, people remain free moral agents. What they do with the witness of Jesus is still their personal choice. But we will have become more "conformed to the likeness of His Son" (see Romans 8:29) and made to be better testimonies of the Gospel. We still won't be perfect until we reach the other side, but the world will recognize that we are "a peculiar people." We're agents of change representing the God Who created mankind and loved us so much that He gave His one and only Son to die for our sins, then rise from the dead. Christ's life, death, and resurrection provide the promise of eternal life to all who will put their faith in Him.

The prayers of God's people have opened the door for a mighty move of God in America more than once in our history, and can do so again. Both individual prayer and corporate prayer are potent weapons against the wiles of the devil. Our petitions before the throne of God can be the catalyst for a national revival again in our lifetime. Repentance and prayer can bring an outpouring of the Holy Spirit down from Heaven itself.

James 5:16-18 presents that fact, and provides an example from the Old Testament. "The prayer of a righteous man is powerful and effective. Elijah was a man just like us. He prayed earnestly that it would not rain, and it did not rain on the land for three and a half years. Again he prayed, and the heavens gave rain, and the earth produced its crops." In the aftermath of a drought brought on by Israel turning away from the Lord, Elijah's prayer resulted in a massive downpour restoring divine blessing on the land! And God can do it again!

The spiritual realm is the greatest area in which we can have a godly affect on our country, but is not the only sphere of influence where we as the church can make an impact. We can attempt to, at least in some measure, take back the three major institutions of society that have been negatively transformed and used to turn America away from the God whose hand was so active in our creation as a nation. We can attempt to enter the existing corrupted entities of education, media, and government to try to help turn them back toward the good.

To some degree some of us have already worked on that, but our impact has often been limited by two factors. Number one, instead of being instruments of change for the good, many Christians have conformed to the godless culture which took over these institutions in the first place. Number two, even when we stand up for what is right, we may be blocked by those in control of these organizations, and thus be unable to affect any positive change from within.

But there are success stories in such scenarios. Abraham stood faithful to God's covenant, and was once able to rescue Sodom and Gomorrah through an army that consisted of trained of soldiers from his own household, and others from his alliance with his friends. Some of his later descendants were also powerful holy influences in the midst of otherwise unholy entities. Joseph became second in command in Egypt, resulting in the salvation of that people and his own. Daniel rose to positions of godly influence and authority in the Babylonian and Medo-Persian empires, benefiting both foreigners and his own people.

On the other hand, because of his compromising, Lot was unable to wield the kind of influence that could move his community to repentance and conversion to Yahweh. He wasn't even able to have spiritual impact to the extent that he should have within his own family.

Another means of taking back these first two powerful fields of communication is to create new organizations in these domains, in order to counteract the existing ones that have been corrupted by sin. We've already done that to an extent through our creation of Christian educational institutions and Christian media outlets. I would love to see us do even more of that. Not all of us have the callings or giftings to work directly in these areas, but those who do should prayerfully consider such action.

Once more we encounter examples of success and failure in this kind of arena through the lives of Abraham and Lot. Abraham and the nations which eventually grew from his loins and his spirit exercised transformational influence upon members of all peoples on earth as long as they remained faithful to the divine covenant. Through his wanderings, however, Lot allowed two nations from his offspring to be established which often stood in the way of God's people entering and fully enjoying the land promised to them.

Even if we aren't directly involved in any of those educational and media fields, at the very least we can exercise our right as citizens to run for public office and to vote in elections for candidates who stand for what is right. By getting so involved we can do our part to try to win the country's government back. Too many believers have failed to vote because they think politics is a dirty game, and thus should be avoided by Christians. Some have felt it just isn't important enough an activity with which to be bothered. Still others think government should have nothing to do with religion, and so they shouldn't take old-fashioned Bible values into the voting booth with them. God help us!

In Hosea Chapter 8 the Lord indicted the people of Israel for breaking His covenant with them and rebelling against His law. In verse 4 He lamented: "They set up kings without my consent; they choose princes without my approval." Isn't that what the United States... even to a large degree American Christians... have done? Like Israel we "...have sown the wind, and... shall reap the whirlwind" (verse 7). We can't always find candidates who stand for *all* that is right, but we can at least choose the ones who come closest to Bible standards.

Charles Finney, the leading preacher of this country's second great awakening, spoke pointedly to believers about their obligations when it comes to elections. "The time has come that Christians must vote for honest men and take consistent ground in politics or the Lord will curse them... Christians have been exceedingly guilty in this matter. But the time has come when they must act differently... Christians seem to act as if they thought God did not see what they do in politics. But I tell you He does see it – and He will bless or curse this nation according to the course they [Christians] take [in politics]."

We also need to be very prayerful and discerning concerning organizations and movements purporting to represent what seem to be righteous causes. Jesus told His followers to "Watch out for false prophets. They come to you in sheep's clothing, but inwardly they are ferocious wolves" (Matthew 7:15). The Apostle Paul further advises believers to beware of deceitful individuals and groups. "...For Satan himself masquerades as an angel of light. It is not surprising, then, if his servants masquerade as servants of righteousness. Their end will be what their actions deserve" (II Corinthians 11:14,15). Don't be quick to join, or even simply lend vocal support to, such trends and associations simply because they're considered politically correct. Examine their philosophies and actions carefully and let the Lord and His Word always be your guide.

If America is ever to come back to the God who has so abundantly blessed us in the past, the Body of Christ must lead the way. Are we willing to do so? Are we willing to pay the price? Millennia ago one righteous man named Lot appears to have been unwilling to do so. His hometown paid an awful penalty for their rebellion against God and His commands. Another righteous man was willing to make a difference. Abraham's military action a few years before their final destruction saved their king, their citizens, and their possessions for a time. Later He passionately interceded with the Lord for their salvation, but their wicked society had by that time gone too far and they refused to repent.

Will America come home to a holy God who loves us, or reject His pleas and ultimately face His wrath? Will we as the church be wanderers like Lot and lose not only our community to divine judgment, but our families to the wicked influence of a culture of sin, or even to death? Or will we stand for the Lord and His righteousness like faithful Abraham? Like the Lord Jesus Himself we must be willing to speak out boldly against sin. Some people will call us haters, but God will call us good and faithful servants. By doing so we can be instrumental in saving a society at large from the destructive power of evil, and its individual citizens from the harm it brings them in this earthly life, and the unimaginable suffering of an eternity in hell in the life to come.

Abraham may not have been able through his prayers to bring salvation to Sodom and Gomorrah because of their unwillingness to turn to God, but his devout walk with the Lord extended the blessings of divine covenant to a nation of his descendants for millennia. And his personal faithfulness to that covenant would enable God to proclaim: "...*all peoples on earth* will be blessed through you" (Genesis 12:3).

As we, the *church in America,* ardently seek the Lord, may our holy lives and fervent prayers serve as the catalyst for a return to the faith of our fathers in the *American nation.* Like the Israelites who returned to the Promised Land after 70 years of captivity in Babylon, may we be able to celebrate the restoration of "one nation under God." I close with the joyful song of God's people on that glorious historical occasion of their homecoming. It's found in Psalm 126. God grant that it may someday soon be our song here in the United States!

"When the LORD brought back the captives to Zion, we were like men who dreamed. Our mouths were filled with laughter, our tongues with songs of joy. Then it was said among the nations, 'the LORD has done great things for them.' The LORD has done great things for us, and we are filled with joy. Restore our fortunes, O LORD, like streams in the Negev. Those who sow in tears will reap with songs of joy. He who goes out weeping, carrying seed to sow, will return with songs of joy, carrying sheaves with him."

About the Author

Sam Mason's love for God and His Word began as a result of his upbringing in a home rich with the godly influence of loving Christian parents. Over the years that early impartation of faith has only grown as he's continued to study and proclaim the truths of Scripture. A graduate of what is now Northpoint Bible College, Sam has been a preacher, teacher, counselor, author, singer, and songwriter. He's served many years in pastoral ministry and Christian broadcasting. Now retired from full-time work, he and his wife, Carol, live in Virginia. In addition to some preaching, teaching, and volunteer work, he spends much of his time writing.

Printed in the United States
by Baker & Taylor Publisher Services